· MALA POWERS ·

Follow the Year

A Family Celebration of Christian Holidays

Illustrated by Frances Elizabeth Livens

Harper & Row, Publishers, San Francisco

Cambridge, Hagerstown, New York, Philadelphia
London, Mexico City, São Paulo, Singapore, Sydney

FOLLOW THE YEAR. *A Family Celebration of Christian Holidays.*
Text copyright © 1985 by Mala Powers.
Illustration copyright © 1985 by Frances Livens.
All rights reserved. Printed in Italy by New Interlitho S.p.A., Milan.
No part of this book may be used or reproduced in any manner
whatsoever without written permission except in the case of brief
quotations embodied in critical articles and reviews.
For further information address Harper & Row, Publishers, Inc.,
10 East 53rd Street, New York, NY 10022.

FIRST U.S. EDITION

LC# 85-42791

ISBN: 0-06-06669305

85 86 87 88 89 10 9 8 7 6 5 4 3 2 1

7087388

For Toren, Anna, Damion and Liv Sara . . . who represent all the children everywhere! With special thanks to my husband, M. Hughes Miller, for his invaluable help and understanding.

Contents

Christmas Festival

Easter Festival

Festival of John the Baptist

Michaelmas Festival

Introduction

In writing this book, I hope to help today's Christian family — whatever their particular denomination — to understand and follow the rhythm of the Christian festivals through the course of the entire year. The celebration of these festivals serves both to strengthen the family as a whole and greatly enrich the life of each individual.

Beautifully and sensitively illustrated by Frances Elizabeth Livens, FOLLOW THE YEAR hopes to speak to the heart about God's rhythms and seasons which weave through all His created world. It combines biblical stories and legends with modern tales and explains the meanings and origins of many of the festivals. The book also describes celebrations associated with these holy-days, looking at fascinating customs from all over the world and providing moving and entertaining festival tales which will be enjoyed by both children and grown-ups alike.

FOLLOW THE YEAR does not attempt to give a complete picture of the traditional Christian year with all its festivals and seasons. Instead, it concentrates on those more meaningful and interesting ones which fall near the solstices and equinoxes: those great pillars of the year which usher in our four seasons. Nature's ever changing seasons are the stage upon which the drama of all the festivals unfold.

FOLLOW THE YEAR is not only a book about Christian festivals to be read and absorbed passively; it also encourages active involvement. Since the publication of my previous book, FOLLOW THE STAR, a Christmas Advent-ure, I have received hundreds of heart-warming messages from families who now enjoy Advent prayers and story-telling celebrations in their homes. They speak of a growing sense of family closeness which comes from these gatherings. FOLLOW THE YEAR also encourages family celebrations . . . not only at Christmas but during Easter, Michaelmas and the mid-summer Festival of John the Baptist.

Throughout this book there are suggestions as to how the family may actually participate in these holy seasons. Festivals are not just religious occasions but social as well; times for feasting and exchanging gifts. And they should be fun — especially for children! Acting out a simple scene from a Nativity play; making an Advent wreath; decorating Easter eggs . . . these are just some of the ways in which parents can encourage their children to appreciate the *theme* of each festival. My experience has shown that they will also be helping their children feel a closer relationship with their Christian faith. As one little girl told me, "Jesus smiles when we make things to 'member His days."

Most importantly, through the conscious celebration of these rhythmic festivals we come to an ever deepening experience of God the Father, God the Son and God the Holy Spirit. For God, who speaks to us through all things, speaks especially loudly and forcefully through the rhythms of the year.

Mala Powers

North Hollywood, California

Follow the Year

Follow the year the Lord has made,
Follow His seasons and rounds,
He made the sun and the stars and the earth,
In their rhythms His glory abounds.

As we journey through the year we find that everywhere, in the world around us and within ourselves, there are rhythms and cycles through which God is always working and revealing His secrets. We observe the movements of our earth, the sun, the moon and the stars and their relations to one another. They bring us night and day, light and darkness, warmth and cold and the glories that come with the changing seasons. Within each and every human being these same mighty rhythms are also at work. The calendar of the Christian year, too, is composed of cycles and rhythms — the Christian seasons with their festivals — which bring to us powerful images that can deepen our love and understanding of Jesus Christ.

Rhythms of the Christian Year

During hundreds of years, the calendar for the Christian year emerged with its seasons and festivals, octaves, tides and saints' days. As different Christian demoninations came into being, the calendar was re-formed and simplified. Today, every denomination adapts and uses its own variation of the Christian calendar.

Celebrating Christian festivals throughout the year can be thought of as holding a great and regular conversation with God. The first half of the traditional Church year (Advent to Whitsun) emphasises God speaking to Man through revelation. It *reveals* the nature of God through the life of Jesus Christ; His birth, death, Resurrection, Ascension and His sending of the Holy Spirit.

The second half of the Christian year falls after Whitsun. It focuses attention on Man responding to God — on what Man will make of what he has been given.

This second half of the year, which includes the Festival of John the Baptist and Michaelmas, concentrates on the teachings of Christian life. These encourage Man to *respond* to God in a creative manner — through commitment, through prayer and faith, through works performed in love, and through striving to understand how Christ is continually working within each of us.

Rhythms in Nature

The background for the celebration of Christian festivals is the changing scenery of the four seasons as they occur in the northern hemisphere. Yet, the earth's cycle of the year is much more than a mere background. The Gospel of John tells us that Christ, the word of God, was with God from the beginning and that 'all things were made by Him'. The rhythms at work in the life of the earth and its seasons were created by Him too. There is great value in *feeling* our way into these seasonal rhythms as we celebrate the Christian festivals: the bleakness of winter; the budding of spring; the flowering and fruiting of summer and the dying plant life in autumn which makes possible the bursting forth of new life once again in the spring. Through this *feeling* for nature, we become more open to receive and understand the Divine which is constantly at work in us and in our universe.

ADVENT

Through twenty-four daily stories, legends, poems and the Gospel we prepare for Christmas.

CHRISTMAS

Heartwarming Christmas stories old and new help celebrate the Birth of Jesus.

THANKSGIVING

We give thanks for a fruitful year before starting anew with Advent cheer.

HALLOWE'EN

The history and celebration of All Souls' Day and All Hallows' Eve — 'Hallowe'en'.

MICHAELMAS

Archangel Michael legends inspire men with courage to be God's helpers on earth.

JOHN THE BAPTIST'S DAY

Traditions and celebrations renew devotion to God amid summer beauty and joy.

WHITSUN

Customs and events which tell about the Descent of the Holy Spirit to Christ's disciples.

DEC

NOV

OCT

AUTUMN

SEPT

AUG

JULY

SUMMER

CHRISTMASTIDE

Stories, legends and customs to celebrate the twelve days between Christmas and Three Kings' Day.

LENT

Preparing for Easter with inspirational stories, activities and Easter symbols.

WINTER
JAN
FEB
MAR
SPRING
APR
MAY
JUN

EASTERTIDE/ASCENSION

For these forty days — legends and Bible stories of the Risen Christ and His disciples.

EASTER

The story of the Resurrection of Christ retold from the Gospels.

Good Ga-bri-el, Archangel Great,
Helps cleanse our world of strife and hate,
As Gospel Words root, bud and flower —
And in our hearts become Love-power,
God's Herald of our Saviour's birth
Aids us to do His will on earth.

The Christmas Story

According to the Gospel of Luke

And it came to pass in those days, that there went out a decree from Caesar Augustus, that all the world should be taxed. And all went to be taxed, every one into his own city. And Joseph also went up from Galilee, out of the city of Nazareth, into Judaea, unto the city of David, which is called Bethlehem; (because he was of the house and lineage of David:) to be taxed with Mary his espoused wife, being great with child.

And so it was, that, while they were there, the days were accomplished that she should be delivered. And she brought forth her firstborn son, and wrapped him in swaddling clothes, and laid him in a manger; because there was no room for them in the inn.

And there were in the same country shepherds abiding in the field, keeping watch over their flock by night. And, lo, the angel of the Lord came upon them, and the glory of the Lord shone round about them: and they were sore afraid.

And the angel said unto them, Fear not: for, behold, I bring you good tidings of great joy, which shall be to all people. For unto you is born this day in the city of David a Saviour, which is Christ the Lord. And this shall be a sign unto you; Ye shall find the babe wrapped in swaddling clothes, lying in a manger. And suddenly there was with the angel a multitude of the heavenly host praising God, and saying, Glory to God in the highest, and on earth peace, good will toward men.

Luke 2:1-14

The Christmas Advent-ure

It is not far to Bethlehem:
The shortest cut I know
Is that directly through the heart,
The way that children go.

It is not far to Bethlehem:
It cannot take you long,
It is no farther than a prayer
The distance of a song.

Ulrich Troubetzkoy

The Birthday of Jesus of Nazareth, celebrated each year near the winter solstice, directs our thoughts toward the whole mystery of birth. Through finding a few moments each day to meet together as a family to celebrate the Christmas season, we can truly open our hearts to receive the thrill of the Holiest of all Births which took place on that first Christmas morning.

The exact birthdate of Jesus Christ is not known but during the fifth century the date of December 25 was chosen for the Feast of the Nativity, our Christmas. By the sixth century a period of pre-Christmas preparation had been established as beginning on the fourth Sunday before Christmas Day. The name given to that time was 'Advent' which means 'coming' or 'coming in'.

The early Christians made *word-pictures* of the way in which the earth and all God's creatures rejoice at this 'coming in'. These word-pictures are called legends, and even today they still speak to our hearts. Legends relate how flowers magically burst into bloom on the night of Jesus' birth; how animals everywhere kneel to pray at the stroke of midnight on Christmas Eve; and how the sun dances in the sky at dawn on Christmas morn. They describe how ancient trees, bent with age, straightened themselves, put on new leaves and gave forth the fragrance of blossoms at His birth. They tell how even the stones were glad, and old Mother Earth herself rejoiced that through His coming she was made young again.

In our modern age we have many ways to celebrate the period of His 'coming in'; as many different ways as there are different families. Choosing a favourite prayer to be said each day — telling or reading a Bible passage, a Christmas story or legend — playing and singing Christmas carols — opening another window on an Advent Calendar — making an Advent wreath — these are only a few suggestions.* It doesn't matter *how* we choose to celebrate, if only we will take the few wonderful moments of peace and joy which are necessary to remember that Christmas means the birth of Jesus Christ. There is a child within each one of us, no matter what our age, who will soon feel that once again this year *something wonderful is about to happen!* We will find that we are involved in a great Christmas Advent-ure. And when at last Christmas comes, we will be able to welcome the new born Jesus Christ with all the love in our hearts.

Little Christ-Child, come to me,
Let my heart Thy shelter be;
Such a home Thou will not scorn.
So the bells on Christmas morn,
Glad shall ring, "A Christ is born!"

Kate Louise Brown

*For additional ideas see page 122

Stories for Advent

Stories to tell for the twenty-four days of Advent

Day 1—The Advent Wreath

The Advent wreath with candles bright
Helps us prepare for Holy Night.
As old, wise carols now resound
And Christmas symbols here abound,
If only we will search and see,
They all reveal a mystery;
Through every candle, tree and stone
God speaks — and makes great secrets known.

The Advent wreath is always round,
No start or finish can be found.
Like God's eternal love for men
There's no beginning and no end.
Our wreath is made of evergreens,
Can we discover what that means?

Four candles on our wreath we find
A wealth of lore they bring to mind.
For special are the weeks ahead
Till Christ comes to his manger-bed;
And if each day we do our part
We'll build that manger in our hearts.

One candle we will light today
To welcome Jesus on his way.
Next week a second flame will gleam
To be like him becomes our dream.
The third week one more light we'll add;
He'll soon be here to make us glad!
In Christmas week four candles shine;
The Christ Child's near! He's yours! He's mine!

Day 2 — The Double Christmas Gift

John, a young African boy, listened carefully as his teacher explained why it is that Christians give presents to one another at Christmas. "The gift is an expression of our joy over the birth of Jesus and of our friendship for one another," she said.

When Christmas Day came, John brought the teacher a seashell of lustrous beauty. "Where did you ever find such a beautiful shell?" the teacher asked as she gently fingered the gift.

John told her that there was only one spot where such extraordinary shells could be found. When he named the place, a certain bay several miles away, the teacher was left almost speechless.

"Why it's gorgeous — wonderful — but you shouldn't have gone all that way to get a gift for me."

His eyes brightening, the African boy answered, "Long walk part of gift."

Day 3 — Man in the Likeness of God

God the Father, God the Son and God the Holy Spirit said, "Let us make man in our own image and likeness to have dominion over all the earth."

And God poured forth His great love as He created Mankind, and the Heavenly Host brought to man seed-gifts from fruits they had received from God the Father. They brought the seeds of Strength, Love, Wisdom, Freedom and much, much more!

At last Man was created and within him were the seeds of all he would become; seeds that must grow and be nourished, not in Heaven, but upon the earth. And Man was called Adam, meaning 'Man of Earth'.

Then the Heavenly Host marvelled at Adam's magnificent appearance! The form of his face was like that of the sun and his eyes shone like the sun and the light of his body was as a gleaming crystal.

And with love, God placed Adam in the Paradise Garden of Eden.

Inspired by old Christian and Hebrew stories of the Creation

Day 4 — The Fall From Paradise

God walked and talked with Adam and Eve in the Garden of Eden and in this Paradise, where there was no death, He gave them all that they needed. But God warned Adam and Eve not to eat from *one* tree — the Tree of the Knowledge of Good and Evil.

Then the Devil, who had rebelled against God, plotted to gain control of Man and, as the wily serpent, he tempted Eve. He told her to eat from the forbidden tree so that she would become wise. Eve wanted to be wise — and after taking a bite of the shiny fruit from the forbidden tree she persuaded Adam also to eat the fruit.

At once they saw things differently. They felt naked and ashamed. They tried to hide from God. But God knew that they had eaten of the forbidden fruit and He told Adam and Eve that they must leave Paradise. Man would now have to earn salvation. He would know toil, evil, pain and death until with love and freedom he learned to choose good above evil.

But the task was too hard for Man alone;
Only God, Himself, could help Man atone.
And God in His wisdom wove a great plan,
A plan which thousands of years would span —
For part of Himself to be born in Man —
And the journey of Christ to earth began.

Adapted from the Book of Genesis

Day 5 — St. Nicholas' Eve

December 5

On the evening before December 6, children in many European countries eagerly await a visit from St. Nicholas — for in those lands it is the good St. Nicholas who brings gifts to children rather than Father Christmas, Santa Claus or the Three Kings. Sometimes St. Nicholas visits openly, at family gatherings, and other times he comes unseen while children are asleep! Like Santa Claus and Father Christmas he is generous with sweets and presents — if the children have been good.

For centuries St. Nicholas has been loved and revered. Born in Asia Minor in the fourth century A.D., he became a Bishop at a very young age. Stories and legends of his great compassion and generosity spread rapidly. One story tells how he came to help a family so poor that the eldest of three daughters was about to be sold into slavery. Twice, unseen by anyone, Nicholas dropped a bag of gold through their window to provide marriage dowries for two of the daughters. But as Nicholas secretly tried to leave gold a third time, he was discovered! "Promise never to tell anyone of this!" Nicholas insisted. And ever after, the legends tell, many of the best gifts of St. Nicholas have been left in secret!

Day 6 — The Little Stranger

In the cottage of a poor woodcutter on a cold Christmas Eve, two children sat with their mother and father by the fire. Suddenly they heard a soft knocking at the door.

"Come in, come in!" cried the family when they saw the shivering, ragged little child who stood outside in the darkness.

They quickly wrapped the child in a blanket and sat him near the fire. They shared their food with him and, when he fell asleep, the children gave him their bed and slept on the floor near the fire.

In the night they were awakened by the beautiful sound of music and, looking out, they saw a band of singing angels. In their midst was the little stranger, no longer dressed in rags, but in shining garments made of silvery light. They knew at once it was the Christ Child.

"Each year I wander through the world to bring peace, joy and warmth to the hearts of those who will receive me," said the Child. Then He broke a branch from a small fir tree and planted it in the snow. At once a tree grew, and delicious fruit appeared upon its branches. "As you have fed and cared for me," He said with a radiant smile, "so shall this tree give fruit for your souls each year on the Eve of my birthday."

Retold from a Bavarian legend

14

Day 7 — The Annunciation

"Mary, Oh Mary! Your praises we sing.
God chose you to mother our dear little King."

In the small town of Nazareth lived Mary, a maiden so pure, so full of light, that there was no darkness in her. She loved God and wanted to do His will.

On a wondrous day, a great light suddenly filled Mary's room and the Angel Gabriel appeared and said, "Hail Mary! Do not be afraid. You have found favour with God. The Holy Spirit shall come to you and you shall bring forth a son — Jesus — and He shall be called the Son of God."

Mary wondered at this for she was not yet married to Joseph. Still, she bowed her head and said, "In everything I shall serve the will of the Lord."

And so the first great Advent began. Mary waited — 'pondering in her heart' the mystery of the great gift God was sending to her and to the world. Mary waited — she prayed and gave thanks, preparing herself to wisely raise this Holy Child. And now, nearly two thousand years later, *we* wait — *we* pray and give thanks, preparing a birthplace within our hearts where the Christ Child can be born again each year.

Adapted from the Gospel of Luke

Day 8 — The Christ Child and the Birds of Clay

Six-year-old Jesus had just fashioned a number of delicate birds from some wet potter's clay. "Look, Mother," Jesus called out, "see the colours of the sunrise in this bowl of water!" Then Jesus dipped His fingers into the coloured water and with the reflected sunbeams clinging to His fingers, He gently painted each clay bird with lustrous colours.

"How blessed and wondrous is my son!" thought Mary and after kissing the boy, returned to her work and pondered in her heart what she had seen. Suddenly the village bully appeared at Jesus' side and, without warning, grabbed up one of the birds and squeezed it into a shapeless blob of clay. "Don't do that," Jesus cried out. "Birds are made to fly!" And as the bully laughed mockingly, Jesus swiftly thrust the clay birds up towards the sky saying, "Fly, birds, fly!"

Then before the bully's astonished eyes, the clay birds took life and began to flap their wings and fly. The village boy looked with awe at Jesus. Overcome by a sudden feeling of shame, he dropped his gaze. It was then that he noticed one small clay bird, still lying on the ground. Gently he picked it up and handed it to Jesus. "Please make it fly, too," he said.

A moment later all the birds, perched in a nearby tree, sang their thanks. And both the boy, who was no longer a bully, and the young Christ Child clapped their hands in glee!

Adapted from the Apocrypha

Day 9 — The Glastonbury Thorn

At Glastonbury it is told,
By bard and pilgrim songs of old,
Each Christmas Eve at midnight hour
Good Joseph's hawthorn staff does flower —
Acclaiming that all things of earth
This night shall honour our Lord's birth!

Legend tells us that in the early years of Christianity, Joseph of Arimathea, who had reverently taken the body of Jesus from the cross and laid it in the tomb, sailed to Glastonbury, England. Fair Glastonbury was then an orchard isle — thought to be King Arthur's island of Avalon. There, just before Christmas, good Joseph thrust his hawthorn staff, brought with him from Jerusalem, into the earth, claiming it as Holy Ground for the Lord. By Christmas Eve the staff had miraculously taken root and burst into blossom! Each year thereafter, it continued to flower on Christmas Eve. For centuries pilgrims have come from everywhere to see this wondrous Christmas blooming.

During the Puritan rule, the original hawthorn was cut down but, fortunately, grafts and cuttings from the original tree had taken root nearby. Even today, if you visit the Abbey grounds at Glastonbury, you will find, still blossoming, a thorn tree grown from the shoot of Joseph's Glastonbury thorn.

Adapted from old French and English legends

Day 10 — The Animals' Christmas

Jesus was born in a stable, with the animals' manger for His bed. In many countries animals are remembered at Christmas with special 'treats'. In Norway, hunting and fishing ceases for a time so that all of God's creatures may know the 'Peace of Christmas'.

The legendary deeds and stories of our animal friends are part of Christmas celebrations in every land. One old legend tells that every Christmas Eve, just at the stroke of midnight, the barnyard animals all kneel to adore our little Lord and receive the power of speech to tell again of the Holy Birth.

In folklore, the birth of Jesus is honoured by *all* God's creatures. Bees are said to hum their own special hymn of praise. Even the little spiders, taken pity on by the Christ Child, were allowed to spin their gossamer webs upon the Christmas tree. At a touch from the Holy Child, their cobwebs turned to silver threads.

Many of our Christmas gift bringers have animal helpers. St. Nicholas rides a white horse, the Three Kings ride horses or camels and Santa Claus, of course, with his sleigh full of toys, is carried high over the house tops by flying reindeer.

Adapted from legends of many lands

Day 11 — Legend of the Poinsettia

It was Christmas Eve and outside the small Mexican church a little girl, Lola, wept and prayed:

"Oh please, Lord, help me! I have not even a small flower-gift to place beside the manger to show the Baby Jesus how much I love him."

Suddenly, in a brilliant light, Lola saw her Guardian Angel beside her.

"The Holy Child knows you love Him, Lola — He sees the many kind deeds you do for others. Gather those plants that grow beside the road."

"But they are weeds!" exclaimed Lola.

"Weeds are only plants for which man has not yet discovered God's purpose," said the Angel with a smile.

Lola entered the church carrying the straggly greens and reverently laid them among the many flowers placed by villagers around the manger.

Suddenly gasps of astonishment echoed throughout the church as Lola's 'weeds' changed into the most beautiful flame-red flowers!

Since that day, these flowers are known in Mexico as the *Flores de la Noche Buena* — the Christmas Flowers.

Adapted from a Mexican legend

Day 12 — Legend of the Birds

The gleaming black raven, it is told, was the first to hear of the birth of our little Lord. As he flew at night over the gentle hills near Bethlehem, angels appeared and told him the wondrous news! At once he took the joyous news to all the birds.

Through the ages, since the star first lighted the sky over Bethlehem and the birth of the Christ Child, legends, poems, carols and stories have reminded us of the devotion of birds to the Holy Family.

The stork, it is said, flew to the stable as soon as she heard the news and plucked the feathers from her own breast to make a soft and downy pillow for the Holy Child. Then came the tiny wren who carefully wove a blanket of tender leaves to cover Him. The doves cooed and the nightingale sang its sweetest lullabye, all the night long, to soothe the Babe into sleep so that He might dream of Heaven on His first night on earth.

Adapted from legends of many lands

Day 13 — Santa Lucia's Day

December 13

There is a legend that once, during a time of great hunger in Sweden, Santa Lucia, her head surrounded by a halo of light, miraculously appeared and provided the country with food.

Today in Sweden on December 13 you would probably see many young girls wearing halos of lighted candles on their heads. For on this date, every city, office, church and school chooses its own young girl as the 'Lucia Bride'.

In most Swedish homes, too, there is a 'Lucia'. Very early in the morning, a young Elsa slips out of bed. She dresses in a sparkling white dress with a bright red sash. Her mother helps to light the seven candles on Elsa's crown of evergreens. Then Elsa, as the Lucia Bride, serves coffee and special 'Lucia Cakes' to the family.

Santa Lucia's day originally fell on the shortest day of the year and, like all Festivals of Light, was celebrated with candles and fire to drive away the cold darkness and to welcome the returning sunlight. No wonder that Sweden loves their candle-crowned Lucia and begins its Christmas celebrations with her day.

Adapted from Swedish legends and customs

Day 14 — God's Crowning Creation

God had created the world and everything in it — from the least worm in the dust to the crowning glory of creation — Man.

The Angels were astounded by Man's beauty, but some could not understand why God had made Man. What need had God for Man on earth when heaven was so full of Angels. They talked about this among themselves and at last decided to ask God himself. One small Angel stepped up to the throne of God and asked, "Heavenly Father, you have a heaven full of Angels, great and small. So why did you create Man?"

When God the Father heard this He called all the Angels to Him. Then He bent down to the earth, and picked a red rose whose petals had opened; "Who will tell me," God asked the Angels, "what I am holding in my hand?"

But not one of the countless Angels could name what God was holding. They stood silent about His throne and could give no answer.

Then God the Father said: "I created Man so that there should be one being in the world who *knows* what God the Father has created, and would give it a name for all of us to remember."

Adapted from a Norwegian story by Dan Lindholm

Day 15 — The Shepherd's Flute

The Gospels tell of the Angels' message to the shepherds on that first Christmas Eve — but what of a young shepherd off searching for a lost sheep? A Scandinavian legend tells that he, too, saw an Angel who told him the great news and gave the boy a gift — a flute with seven pure notes to play a tune for the Holy Child.

Joyously the shepherd lad began his journey to Bethlehem, but when he tripped and fell on the rocky road, the flute flew from his hand. The boy swore in anger and when he picked up the flute, one note had been lost. Soon after, a snarling wolf appeared. The frightened boy flung the flute at the wolf, driving him away. Now the flute could play only five notes.

One by one — through deeds caused by fear or anger — more precious notes were lost, until when at last he reached the open stable door, only one note was left in the flute.

Ashamed that so little of his gift remained, the shepherd boy felt he could not approach the Holy Babe. He did not know that each of us comes to the Redeemer feeling much like this.

Mary saw the boy and beckoned him forward. Quietly he approached the Child and putting the flute to his lips played its last, its one and only, note. It still had a marvellous purity and the Babe listened! Then the Christ Child put forth his hand and touched the flute. And in that same moment it became whole again, all its notes played clearly and beautifully, just as when it first was sent from Heaven.

Adapted from a Norwegian story
by Dan Lindholm

Day 16 — Picture Gifts

Mr. Jones sadly announced to his children, "There'll be no Christmas presents this year. With God's help there'll be food on the table, but that's all we can manage."

That's when twelve-year-old Tim called all the children into action. "Mother and Dad are worried *for us*," he said, "so let's show them we can still make this a Merry Christmas!"

Later the children gathered before their parents and announced, "Let's give *pictures* of the presents we'd *like* to give each other." They all agreed; and so on Christmas morning, under the picture of a tall Christmas tree, painted on shelf paper, there were heaps of *pictured* riches! For Mother there was a shiny modern stove, jewelled bracelets and earrings, and a beautiful water-colour of an Angel, hand-painted by Sis. For Dad there were cut-out pictures of a sleek green Jaguar sports-car and the 'world's most complete tool kit'. Of course there were dozens of pictures and drawings of toys and games for all the children; and everyone gave their joy and laughter! It was the best Christmas ever — summed up by little Colin's childishly drawn picture of a man, a woman and five children, all holding hands — with the star above them — and under the picture was one word, LOVE!

Day 17 — St. Francis and the Christmas Crèche

The night-time darkness had fled! The woodland clearing on a mountain near the small Italian village of Greccio was made bright as day with torchlight. The villagers cried out in surprise and awe as they beheld the Christmas Eve gift of St. Francis of Assisi. For near a rock cave was a real manger, filled with straw. On one side of the manger stood a large live ox and on the other side, a small grey ass. Their warm breaths turned frosty white in the cold night air.

The chanting of the Franciscan Brothers echoed through the rocky hills as St. Francis stood in front of the manger. Overcome with tenderness, he watched as the villagers saw and felt the cold and poverty of the humble birthplace of the 'Little Brother of all Mankind'. Then with a wondrous joy, St. Francis read aloud from the Holy Gospel.

Since that deeply stirring night near Greccio, the Christmas crèche has become a part of the world's Christmas celebration. And whether as a living dramatisation, a large Nativity scene, or carved miniatures, it brings happiness to the hearts of adult and child alike. Gazing upon the crèche with reverence brings us always closer to the two thousand year old — but ever new — Christmas Mystery.

Adapted from 'Vita Prima' by Thomas Celano (approximately 1258 A.D.)

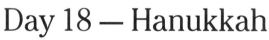

Day 18 — Hanukkah

When Jesus was growing up, He and His family celebrated all the great Hebrew Festivals of the year. In the Hebrew month of *Kislev* (our December) a beautiful Festival of Lights known as 'Hanukkah' is celebrated. Its story is one that Jesus must often have heard.

Israel was once ruled by the cruel Syrian-Greek king Antiochus. He defiled the Holy Temple in Jerusalem. By his order, thousands of Jews were killed because they refused to give up their God and the laws of their religion in order to worship Greek Gods. At last, a Jewish hero, Judas, called the Maccabee, led a rebellion which drove the Syrians from Jerusalem. The Holy Temple was rededicated and the *Ner Tamid,* the 'Eternal Lamp', was relighted. It was then decided that each year at that season, a joyous festival should be held.

Hanukkah is that festival, and during its eight-day celebration candles are lighted, one for each night, in a special candelabra. Hanukkah always falls near and sometimes *on* our Christmas and in more recent times Hanukkah gifts are given, especially to children.

Adapted from the Apocrypha — the Books of the Maccabees

Day 19 — Martin Luther and the Christmas Tree Candles

Of the many Christmas tree stories and legends, a very special one comes from Germany. It tells about Martin Luther, the great leader of the Reformation movement in the church about five hundred years ago.

One December night, the story tells, Martin Luther was on his way home through the woods. The night was especially bright and clear and thousands of stars twinkled and shimmered in the sky, like windows through which the light of heaven streamed down upon the earth. With joy Martin Luther beheld how the starlight touched the snow-laden boughs of the forest fir trees, making their ice crystals glisten like diamonds.

Deeply moved, Luther decided to share his glimpse of this meeting of heaven and earth! He selected a small, fragrant fir tree and hurried home to his wife and children. There he tied little white candles to the tree's branches; and when they were lit, Martin Luther spoke to his children about the beauty of the stars shining upon the earth and of the Glory of our Heavenly Father who gave Jesus Christ to us to be the Light of the World.

Adapted from a German legend

Day 20 — The 'Luck Boy' of Toy Valley

At Christmas time shops everywhere display wonderful wooden toys from certain small villages in Austria's Tirol mountains. This is how it began.

When young Franz's mother left to work in Vienna, he stayed behind with his grandfather who carved picture frames.

One day Franz received a shiny new carving knife as a 'luck-gift' from his mother. In the Tirol, many years ago, people believed that with a 'luck gift' a child might become 'elf-aided' — that is, elves would lead him to great good fortune! Franz couldn't see what luck could come from a knife, but with the help of his grandfather, Franz began whittling and, with lots of hard work, soon carved a sheep, a lamb, a dog, a lion — until he had a whole animal menagerie.

A young visitor from Vienna, charmed by Franz's animals, bought them all and when other children saw them, orders poured in — more than Franz could fill. Soon other villagers, who until then had carved only picture frames and statues of saints, began to carve animals and toys. The village prospered. And even today, in the Tirol, villagers still speak of the 'elf-aided magic' of hard work; and so praise the 'Luck Boy' of Toy Valley.

Day 21 — Two Doubting Thomases

At one of their nightly pre-Christmas celebrations, nine-year-old Thomas confided to his mother, "I — I love God and Jesus, but sometimes I don't understand — and I have so many doubts!"

Mrs. Craig smiled gently. "I'm so glad you told me, Tom. This is a good time to tell you the story of the *first* 'Doubting Thomas'."

"Thomas was one of the twelve disciples of Jesus — yet, after Jesus' death on the cross, Thomas refused to believe the news that Jesus had really risen from the dead. 'I must see for myself,' he insisted. In spite of Thomas' lack of faith, our Lord came to him. He let Thomas *see* Him and èven *touch* him. And after Jesus Christ had helped Thomas to overcome doubt, Thomas shared his great faith with thousands of people. So you see, Tom, Jesus doesn't turn aside from us just because we doubt or lack faith. He loves us and knows that we *all* need His help to overcome our doubts."

Mother then said this special prayer, "Dear Jesus, we give thanks for the example of Thomas. Help *each of us* to overcome our doubt and to share our faith with others — not only at Christmas time, but always.

Day 22 — A Single Candle Flame

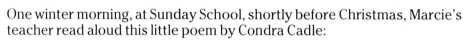

One winter morning, at Sunday School, shortly before Christmas, Marcie's teacher read aloud this little poem by Condra Cadle:

"No deep darkness in the world
Can overcome the light;
A single candle flame will burn
Against the darkest night.
Let all the world of darkness come,
Resentment, envy, fears,
Then light the single flame of love;
The darkness disappears!"

To many children in the class it was only a poem — but for Marcie it was a message. "Perhaps I can light that one little candle flame!" she thought.

At home, Marcie looked through eyes of love at her family. What did each one need to 'light up' some dark spot?

On Christmas Morning Marcie's mother received her small candle and a gift card which read, "As my Christmas gift please take one hour to rest right after dinner on Wednesday and Friday for this whole year! I'll do *all* the dishes!" Then, to her four-year-old brother, Brian, Marcie gave " — a daily story-reading time." And Marcie's card to her Dad promised — one half hour of 'peace and quiet' right after you come home from work each night. *I'll* keep Brian busy!"

As each one opened his gift card, Marcie felt the growing excitement of giving. Brian squealed in delight; Mother hugged her tightly and Dad — well, Dad had just the trace of tears in the corners of his eyes. The whole room was shining with the invisible light of Love.

Day 23 — The Christmas Angel

Starlight streamed in through the frost-covered window and lit up the little Christmas Angel atop the Christmas tree.

"She's beautiful!" whispered Stevie to his sister Carrie as the two tired children drowsed before the Christmas tree. "Do you suppose our Guardian Angels look like that?"

Carrie nodded her agreement. "Only I'm sure a real Angel is a million, million times *more* beautiful! I wish we could see a real Angel." And as the children nodded and dozed, the little Christmas Angel began to shimmer and glow until the real Christmas Angel, as large as the tree itself, stood before the children.

"Carrie," she said with a smile, "you and Stevie have your wish! Tonight your Guardian Angels and I will take you on a special journey."

In the arms of their Guardian Angels, both children were then carried off to a glowing cloud-land, surrounded by shining stars. There they joined many boys and girls and their Guardian Angels who were watching other Angels weaving on a large golden loom.

"Each year Angels weave new garments for the Christ Child to wear when He brings new Heavenly gifts to men on earth," said the Christmas Angel. "The beautiful shimmering threads we weave are the prayers of children who love Jesus and His Heavenly Father."

Soon Carrie and Stevie stood before the golden loom where their prayer-gifts, too, were woven into the garments for the Baby Jesus. Then all the children knelt in prayer and sang a carol for the Christ Child.

Carrie and Stevie were specially blessed for when they awoke they remembered their visit with the Angels. And they gave thanks for the real Angels as they looked up to the figure of the little Christmas Angel on the top of their Christmas tree.

Retold from a European legend

Day 24 — The First Christmas Eve

On this holiest night of the year, come and let's join in a special journey. Our space-and-time ship is our God-gift of imagination, taking us back nearly two thousand years to stand just inside the gate of Bethlehem. The narrow streets are nearly deserted, for it is well past midnight. But look! Before us, just entering the city, is a group of shepherds. How excited they seem — how full of wonder! They hurry along as if led by some invisible guide, and we join them, sharing in their sense of awe. Now we stop at the small entrance of a grotto cave set in a steep hillside. It is a stable!

A man comes quietly forth from the cave and greets the shepherds. The man is Joseph and with a smile he bids the shepherds enter. Humbly we follow. Within the stable we find a young woman, Mary, seated near a manger. How lovely, how soft and glowing is her face. Mary beckons to the shepherds and, with them, we crowd around the manger. There, wrapped in swaddling clothes, lying on the straw, is a new born baby — Jesus! Like no other baby, He is surrounded by a radiance of light in which Angels seem to weave!

The shepherds kneel in rapture. With a rush of feeling, we, too, fall to our knees; for in that moment, light from around the Child enters our hearts. Love flames up within us — Love for the Child, Love for Mary and Joseph, for the shepherds — and for all the earth! The great joyous peace of heaven enfolds us and we hear the sound of Angel voices singing, "Glory to God in the Highest and to men on earth, peace. Peace! For Christ is Born, Christ is Born!"

A Visit from St. Nicholas

'Twas the night before Christmas, when all through the house
Not a creature was stirring, not even a mouse;
The stockings were hung by the chimney with care,
In hopes that St. Nicholas soon would be there;
The children were nestled all snug in their beds
While visions of sugar-plums danced in their heads;
While mamma in her kerchief, and I in my cap,
Had just settled our brains for a long winter's nap, —
When out on the lawn there arose such a clatter,
I sprang from my bed to see what was the matter.

Away to the window I flew like a flash,
Tore open the shutters and threw up the sash.
The moon, on the breast of the new-fallen snow
Gave a lustre of midday to objects below;
When what to my wondering eyes should appear,
But a miniature sleigh and eight tiny reindeer,
With a little old driver, so lively and quick,
I knew in a moment it must be St. Nick.
More rapid than eagles his coursers they came,
And he whistled and shouted, and called them by name:

"Now, Dasher! now, Dancer! now, Prancer and Vixen!
On, Comet! on, Cupid! on, Donner and Blitzen!
To the top of the porch, to the top of the wall!
Now dash away, dash away, dash away, all!"

As dry leaves that before the wild hurricane fly,
When they meet with an obstacle, mount to the sky,
So up to the housetop the coursers they flew,
With the sleigh full of toys, and St. Nicholas too.

And then in a twinkling I heard on the roof
The prancing and pawing of each little hoof.
As I drew in my head, and was turning around,
Down the chimney St. Nicholas came with a bound.

He was dressed all in fur from his head to his foot,
And his clothes were all tarnished with ashes and soot;
A bundle of toys he had flung on his back,
And he looked like a peddler just opening his pack.
His eyes — how they twinkled! his dimples, how merry!
His cheeks were like roses, his nose like a cherry!
His droll little mouth was drawn up like a bow,
And the beard on his chin was as white as the snow.

The stump of a pipe he held tight in his teeth,
And the smoke it encircled his head like a wreath.
He had a broad face and a little round belly
That shook, when he laughed, like a bowl full of jelly.
He was chubby and plump, a right jolly old elf;
And I laughed when I saw him, in spite of myself.
A wink of his eye and a twist of his head
Soon gave me to know I had nothing to dread.

He spoke not a word, but went straight to his work,
And filled all the stockings; then turned with a jerk,
And laying his finger aside of his nose,
And giving a nod, up the chimney he rose.
He sprang to his sleigh, to his team gave a whistle,
And away they all flew like the down of a thistle;
But I heard him exclaim, ere he drove out of sight,
"Happy Christmas to all, and to all a good-night!"

Clement C. Moore

Silent Night

Not a sound would come forth from the pipe organ in the church. Not even a single note! In despair, organist Franz Gruber rushed to tell the priest, Father Joseph Mohr. "Mice have eaten through the bellows! There is no way to repair the organ in time for the Christmas Eve service."

The news struck Father Mohr like a thunderbolt. No music for Christmas Eve . . . in the church of St. Nicholas? That would be unthinkable! The little Bavarian village of Oberndorf lay half-buried in snow. No repairman from the outside world could possibly reach them — and it was already Christmas Eve morning!

"What can we do, what can we do?" wailed Herr Gruber, wringing his hands and pacing up and down.

For a moment Father Mohr, too, was caught by fear and anxiety. Then, suddenly calm, he said, "We will pray!"

Astonished, Franz Gruber stopped pacing. How simple Father Mohr made it all sound! "Why, of course!" he agreed. "We will pray."

The two men embraced and soon parted as Father Joseph Mohr, wearing his warmest coat, set out upon his round of parish calls. There were many calls to make; much help and comfort to be given to the sick and the poor — especially at Christmastide.

Suddenly Father Mohr received a hurried and special summons. In a humble cottage on the outskirts of the village, the woodcutter's wife had just given birth to a child. So, on through the snowdrifts the priest trudged in order to welcome and bless the new baby.

It was early evening when Father Mohr returned home, warmed by the memory of the scene he had witnessed that afternoon; the tiny face of the woodcutter's 'Christmas Eve child', nestled in its mother's arms. His mind wandered back over the centuries to that first Christmas Eve. Vividly he pictured the new born Christ Child, sleeping in His mother's arms. Longing to share this vision with his congregation, Father Mohr took up his pen. Effortlessly, words began to flow and soon, with a new poem in hand, he hurried to his friend, the organist Franz Gruber.

"Franz, dear friend, please write a tune to go with my poem; something simple that can be sung at the midnight service to the accompaniment of a guitar."

"But there is not enough time . . ." protested the organist.

"Have faith," urged Father Mohr, his eyes smiling, "God will provide the melody."

Slowly Franz Gruber read the poem. "Beautiful!" he exclaimed. And as he read and re-read the inspiring words, he began to hum a simple melody. Soon both men were humming, then singing: *"Stille Nacht, Heilige Nacht . . ."*

> Silent Night! Holy Night! All is calm, all is bright!
> Round yon Virgin, Mother and Child,
> Holy Infant so tender and mild,
> Sleep in heavenly peace, Sleep in heavenly peace.

And so it happened that on Christmas Eve in 1818, in the candle-lit church of St. Nicholas, the villagers of Oberndorf in Bavaria were the first to hear this beautiful and moving carol. And now, each year, all over the world, millions of people join in carolling this song to express their joy and love through the words and music of:

> Silent Night, Holy Night . . .
> With the Angels let us sing, Alleluia to our King;
> Christ the Saviour is born, Christ the Saviour is born.

Wonder and Joy

The day dawned bright and clear. The little town of Bethlehem began to awaken. Masters as well as servants rose early on this morning, for the inns were full to overflowing with travellers from all over the land of Israel who had returned to this city of their birth to be taxed and counted by the Romans. Merchants were busy setting up their stalls in the market place, food venders and peddlers, with their curious assortment of wares, were already vieing with each other for the choicest spots near the town centre where the Roman census takers and tax collectors would sit. Soon the inns would begin to empty and the seemingly endless lines of men, women and children would form in front of the Roman officials. Nearly all would be willing to buy *something* — if only to relieve the monotony of the many hours of waiting. Yes, it would be a good day for business! That was all important for who in Bethlehem knew, or would have believed that right in their midst, in a cave used to stable animals — ready to be taxed and counted like themselves — was the new born infant Son of God!

Only a short distance from Bethlehem, down below the olive-tree covered hills, near fields where the sheep grazed — there where the humble shepherds and their families lived — this day was quite different.

"Have you heard the news?" an amazed and excited Rachel asked her friend Esther.

Moments later, after hearing the news, an awe-struck Esther repeated to Ruth, "Last night Reuben and Joshua were with other shepherds in the fields when they were awakened by an Angel of God! The Angel told them that the Saviour is born!"

" — And it must be true — " Ruth further related to Matthew and a group of shepherd families who had gathered round to hear the news, "— it must be true for they found the Babe, just as the Angel from Heaven said they would — wrapped in swaddling clothes, lying in a manger. Imagine! the Saviour, whom our prophets have told us about, who is to bring us freedom and save our people — born in a stable!"

"That just shows it can't be true!" said Simon, the skeptic.

"But it is true!" exclaimed old Reuben who, had joined the group. "I know it is true, for I was there! I saw HIM!" Reuben sank to his knees, once again awed by the magnificence of what he had witnessed. All eyes turned to him — all waited breathlessly to hear what old Reuben would say.

"After the Angels gave us the news and went back to Heaven, I went with Joshua and the other shepherds, fast as we could, to Bethlehem.

27

We found the stable — and a man, name of Joseph, said we could come in. When we told him what the Angel said, he didn't seem even a mite surprised. Inside the stable was this beautiful lady — little more than a girl she was — she smiled at us like an Angel . . . And in the manger was the prettiest, brightest-eyed baby you ever did see. Something happened to everyone of us when we looked at Him. Something so great that we couldn't stand on our feet no more. Our legs just sort of folded and next thing you know, we were on our knees — all of us! I just kept staring at Him — feeling like my heart was going to burst with Love! All at once, that little Baby looked at me — right in the eye. Just that quick, the walls of the cave seemed to disappear and all the blessed Angels of heaven were back again, showing me a picture of the whole world — thousands of years from now. The world was just full of people, all glowing with a kind of light that was made of Love. Everybody was loving and helping everybody else and there in the centre of the world was — HIM — as the Babe and as a grown Man — all rolled into one — and they were shining like the sun — like the Lord Hi'self!"

Overcome with emotion as he relived his vision, Reuben could no longer speak. Tears streamed down his face.

Suddenly everyone began talking at once. "We, too, must see the Holy Child — let's go and find the Family." "We'll bring them food," someone shouted. "Sheepskins to keep them warm," cried another.

Old Reuben wiped his eyes and stood up. Smiling, he held up his hand to quiet his friends. "I'll lead you there," he said, "but we must be quiet and careful; only a few of us at a time. His mother needs her rest — and I'm thinking that the Romans should not hear of Him. Not yet!"

And so, all through that First Day, small groups of shepherds and their families, careful not to attract attention, made their way to the stable through the crowds of travellers and tradesmen in the narrow Bethlehem streets. Safely hidden in the folds of their garments were gifts they carried for Him and for Mary and Joseph.

Throughout the day, Mary, holding the Baby Jesus in her arms with Joseph beside her, welcomed their shepherd visitors. How soft and wondering were Mary's eyes as she watched these humble people kneel before her Son and offer their gifts of welcome; bread and milk — a freshly made shepherd's pie — olives and goat's cheese — even the shepherds' own precious luxuries of dates and sweet dried fruit. A little girl brought a bouquet of tiny winter wild flowers and a shepherd lad played a joyous tune on his pipe. One special young boy, whom the others affectionately referred to as 'the clown', told stories. The stories were of nature and simple things, but the boy told them so well and with such gentle humour that Mary laughed aloud, and it seemed to all in the stable that even the Baby Jesus smiled.

And as that day — *the First Christmas Day* — drew to a close and the shepherd groups had taken their leave, the stable seemed still to be full of wonder and joy. Joseph gazed at Mary with love and they gave thanks to the Heavenly Father that there were some — yes, even in the bustling, busy town of Bethlehem — who recognised the Holy Child as their Saviour and rejoiced that He had come. And the Babe, still smiling, drifted into sleep.

> Sleep, Holy Babe,
> Upon thy mother's breast:
> Great lord of earth and sea and sky,
> How sweet it is to see thee lie
> In such a place of rest.
>
> *Edward Caswell*

28

Christmas in Summer

It was Sale-Day in that first week of December back in 1920 when I heard about the Christmas party. That was the day Dad sold Betsy, the roan mare. I'll always remember it because I loved Betsy and I was feeling pretty low. I was only eleven, but on Sale-Days I helped Dad drive the stock into Mooltana, a handful of a place in the far northern end of South Australia.

When I got into the hooded buggy to drive home with Mum, who had come in to do some shopping, I realised it was going to be awfully lonely without the roan mare, especially for Mum. Betsy had really belonged to her and I knew how much Mum cared for her. Still, times were skimpy, and Mum and Dad had talked of selling Betsy for quite a while. Yet, when Mr. Riley bought the roan, I saw Dad's face and it was as long as mine.

Mum drove the buggy through town until we reached Dr. Brenner's house. 'Little Doctor' we called him, and we brought him things from the farm whenever we came into town. "We've made plans for a Christmas party at the Town Hall for the children," Little Doctor announced. "I've asked everyone in the town, but I'd like the farm people to come in too."

Mum said, "A Christmas party! Why, Doctor, I haven't thought about a real Christmas party for years — not since I left England."

Little Doctor's blue eyes twinkled, "It's high time the children around here saw a proper Christmas tree and there's a whole hill of pine trees near by." Mum's cheeks got pink the way they do when she's all stirred up. "Oh, we'd love to come!" she exclaimed.

Little Doctor laughed. "Good! I hope the good Lord will send us a cool day for it," he said as he mopped his face in the boiling heat of the Australian summer.

"This time of the year in England," Mum said softly as we drove home, "when we children came in from school our cheeks and ears were stinging with the lovely icy cold. I'd love to feel that way just once more."

"Funny," I said, "freezing cold there and boiling hot here."

"Just before Christmas," Mum went on, "a pine tree is set up inside the house, and all sorts of glittery, pretty things are hung on it. All around the bottom of the tree presents are heaped, secret presents."

Mum became quiet and I thought about snow and Christmas trees and tidy small villages where people lived close to one another. Suddenly, I started thinking about secret presents. I tasted the word in my mouth. Maybe . . . maybe there was some way I could give Mum a secret present for Christmas. Perhaps I could get Betsy back!

Next day I had to ride over to the Rileys' on an errand for Mum. First off, of course, I told them about the party. Dora Riley, who is only seven, asked, "What's a Christmas tree?" I suppose it seems odd not knowing about Christmas trees, but in the northern part of South Australia it's hot most of the year. December is summer time, and Christmas Day often enough is a fair scorcher. So our families, who are all hard-working farmers and live so far apart, never stopped to put up Christmas decorations.

At the corral, I saw Mr. Riley trying to slip a bridle on Betsy. She kept shying away and by the time he finally got a saddle on her, Mr. Riley was red and sweaty and his temper was short.

Suddenly I felt a warm hope growing inside me. Mr. Riley was an all-right sort of person, and if I explained about a Christmas present for Mum — and if the mare kept on being troublesome — maybe Mr. Riley would sell her back to me.

You see, I had a bit of money of my own. My Gran in England sent me a gold sovereign every birthday, and I'd added quite a little to Gran's money from doing odd jobs.

Ever since I can remember I'd planned that when I had saved enough, I'd buy a black mare that was all my own. I wanted to train her as a high jumper, and win prizes, but this new idea of a 'surprise present' for Mum sort of shunted the little black horse out of my mind.

Several days later I got my chance to talk to Mr. Riley again. He listened quietly while I told him how badly Mum missed the roan mare.

"I know," he said. "Life here is kind of hard on your ma. Still and all, Timmie, I paid good money for the mare."

"I can buy her back," I said, trying to keep my voice steady. "My Gran in England sends me money every birthday."

"Yes, I know," he said. "Want to spend it on your ma, eh, Tim? Well," he grinned, "I've been losing my temper regular with that mare. It's a bargain, Timmie."

We shook hands on it. "I'll ride Betsy into Mooltana," I said, "I'm sure Little Doctor will keep her in his stable till the party."

Back at the farm, I dashed up to my room, and emptied the sovereigns into a small canvas bag. For a minute I felt a little sick inside. It would be a long time before I could think of owning a prize-winning black horse.

On the afternoon of Christmas Eve, Mum and Dad and I climbed into the double-seater buggy for the six-hour drive to Mooltana. The Town Hall is just a plain wooden building, but it didn't look like itself that evening. All the bare windows were garlanded with gum-tree branches and dozens of lanterns were strung across the room. In the centre of the room was a tree!

So that was a Christmas tree! It reached almost to the ceiling, and hundreds of little white wax candles were perched on the branches. Heaps of packages in bright-coloured paper were piled around the bottom.

Little Doctor told us all how he'd tried to make the tree like the one he'd had as a boy. "Only thing," he said, "I couldn't manage the snow for outdoors."

There were presents for everyone, ordered weeks before from Adelaide, over three hundred miles away — tops, paintboxes, balls, books, dolls . . . the o-ohs and a-ahs went around the room in waves. We had supper — sandwiches, milk, cocoa and Christmas cake — and we were the last to leave.

As we reached our buggy, there was Betsy standing beside it — just as I'd planned it. I was shaking with excitement as I went to the mare and handed the reins to Mum.

"It's my Christmas present, Mum," I said. "I bought her back for you."

"Betsy," Mum said softly, "darling Betsy." Then she turned to me, "But I don't understand, Timmie . . . how could you?" Then after a minute she said, "Oh, Timmie, Gran's money . . . you spent Gran's money on me. The money that was to buy the little black horse. Oh, Timmie, Timmie!"

"Gosh, Mum," I said, feeling awkward and funny about it. "I'd rather have Betsy around anyway."

The slow look Dad gave me told me he was pleased with what I'd done. But Mum bent down and kissed me, and her cheek was wet against mine.

On the long ride home to the farm I sat next to Mum on the back seat of the buggy while Betsy clip-clopped along behind us. The Southern Cross sprawled big and brilliant against the sky. I wished that particular moment could last forever.

Next thing I knew, the sky was streaked with pink and gold and Mum was shaking me gently. "Wake up, Timmie dear," she said, "and help your father with the horses. We're home again — *with Betsy* — and it's Christmas Day!"

Abridged from the story by Charlotte Lohse

The Crib of Bo'Bossu

Listen, mes enfants, this is a Noel tale from the northern part of France called Brittany, where lies the ancient walled city of St. Malo.

The people of St. Malo have a famous cathedral built of grey stone. For hundreds of years now, it has been their custom to keep Christmas Eve with a great celebration in the cathedral before beginning the service.

Shortly before midnight, church bells ring out over all the city. In the darkened cathedral, as by some breath of magic, a thousand candles burst into flame and a choir of children, robed in white, break into jubilant song: "Alleluia, Alleluia! Unto us a child is born!"

In front of the nave near the choir a curtain is opened and the manger is disclosed and all may look upon Mary, kneeling by the crib wherein lies the babe, Lord Jesus. Then comes a procession of humble shepherds as the church bells ring out. And so the service begins.

Now in the city of St. Malo, there once lived a young orphan-boy, born — not straight and strong as you and I, but misshapen — with a great hump on his back. Everyone called him Bo'Bossu — the hunchback. He worked as an apprentice to the town's boat-builder. Of all the apprentices none was so skilful or quick with his hands, especially in the delicate task of carving the figureheads which adorned the prows of the large boats. Bo'Bossu was happiest when he worked the wood with tools in his hands — within the safety of the shipyard where he also lived.

But to walk through the streets of St. Malo, that was another matter. For there Bo'Bossu met with other boys, who pelted him with stones or rubbish, called him names and laughed to see the hunchback run.

Yet, not even the stonings or the taunts could keep the orphan, Bo'Bossu, from his beloved cathedral. The Lord Jesus was his brother, and to Him he would bring his aching heart and pour it out in slow, laboured words.

One day as Bo'Bossu was kneeling before the cross, a magnificent idea came to him. He had noticed on the Christmas Eve past, how poor and roughly made was the manger in which the babe, Lord Jesus, lay. Had no one thought to make a better one for the King of Kings? "Oh Lord Jesus," he promised, "I will make Thee a fine crib."

He designed the crib as a little boat, but with two prows, each with an Angel as a figurehead. Bo'Bossu's hours for the boat builder were long and exhausting yet each evening he rushed to the little shed where he lived. Not able to afford candles, Bo'Bossu worked feverishly on the crib until darkness forced him to stop. At dawn he rose again to continue his great work of Love!

Then suddenly, seven days before Christmas, tragedy struck. Everyone was told they must work extra hours — from dawn to dusk each day to finish a new vessel for the fishing fleet. The promised manger remained unfinished!

On Christmas Eve, an exceptionally cold day, work stopped early. Bo'Bossu rushed to his shed and took the unfinished crib from behind his straw bed. The Angel at one prow was not yet carved and there was still much polishing to be done. Fear gripped Bo'Bossu. What of his promise to the Lord!

With frenzied fingers, the hunchback began to carve the Angel. But his hands were like lumps of frozen flesh, He kept dropping his tools — and then the daylight departed! Bo'Bossu could see to work no longer. Exhausted and in despair, he leaned his poor twisted body on the work bench. "I can do no more, Lord, I can do no more!"

Suddenly he felt a hand touch his shoulder and a voice said: "Give me the chisel. Rest. I will do it for you."

The hunchback turned. Beside him stood a boy about his own age. The boy's eyes were as blue as myrtle. The boy's hair was yellow as a candle-flame.

Long they looked at each other, the boy who was whole and the boy who was not. "Can you carve?" asked Bo'Bossu.

"Oh yes; you are very weary, so sleep."

Amazed that he should feel such sudden trust, the exhausted hunchback fell upon his straw bed.

The bells, ringing for the Christmas celebration, wakened him. He jumped up in a panic. "It is too late," he cried, and stumbled over to the work bench. He stood in wonder, for a wide circle of light was about the strange boy, whose hands were giving a last polish to the finished crib. What a marvel of workmanship! Although the crib was of Bo'Bossu's planning and execution, it appeared as if only the hands of the Creator had touched it, making it perfect.

"Who art thou?" asked Bo'Bossu.

"A carpenter's apprentice, even as yourself. I work for my Father," answered the boy. "Come, let us go to the cathedral."

And together they carried the crib that was shaped like a small boat with an Angel at each prow. They entered the church through a side door near to where the manger stood. The boy nodded at Bo'Bossu and said, "Now, lift the Little One into *your* crib, and I will take away the other."

Clumsily the hunchback knelt. Carefully, he laid the Babe into the new boat crib.

Then it was that the greatest of all wonders came to pass. For as Bo'Bossu placed the figure of Lord Jesus in the newly made crib, the Babe opened his eyes and smiled. It was a smile Bo'Bossu knew. The Babe's eyes were as blue as myrtle. His hair was as yellow as a candle-flame.

The hunchback whispered in awe, "Why thou art the boy, and yet not grown as he. The boy is truly thee, and yet not small as thou art." And all the while the Babe kept smiling — the Christ Child — twice come down to earth on that Holy Eve; come down to bless Bo'Bossu, the hunchback.

All at once a thousand candles burst into flame. The curtain before the manger was drawn. The people in the cathedral of St. Malo gasped! For there in the wondrous new manger lay the smiling Babe. And beside the crib was another miracle. Bo'Bossu — yet not the same Bo'Bossu!

From that night, the boy who all his life had been a hunchback walked the streets of St. Malo straight and strong. The people of St. Malo gave him a new name — the name of John, after that favourite disciple of the Lord Jesus. And each Christmas Eve, for many years, the good people of St. Malo pointed to the crib that was like a small boat with an Angel at each end. They told the story of Bo'Bossu to their children and their children's children just as it has been told to you.

Adapted and abridged from the story by Ruth Sawyer

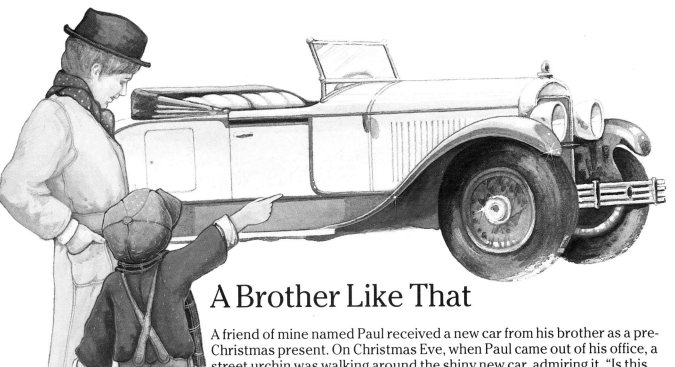

A Brother Like That

A friend of mine named Paul received a new car from his brother as a pre-Christmas present. On Christmas Eve, when Paul came out of his office, a street urchin was walking around the shiny new car, admiring it. "Is this your car, Mister?" he asked.

Paul nodded, "My brother gave it to me for Christmas."

The boy looked astounded. "You mean your brother gave it to you, and it didn't cost you nothing? Gosh, I wish . . ."

He hesitated, and Paul knew what he was going to wish. He was going to wish he had a brother like that. But what the lad said jarred Paul all the way down to his heels. "I wish," the boy went on, "that I could *be* a brother like that."

Paul looked at the boy in astonishment, then impulsively he added, "Would you like to ride in my car?"

"Oh, yes, I'd love that!"

After a short ride the urchin turned, and with his eyes aglow said, "Mister, would you mind driving in front of my house?"

Paul smiled a little. He thought he knew what the lad wanted. He wanted to show his neighbours that he could ride home in a big car. But Paul was wrong again.

"Will you stop right where those two steps are?" the boy asked.

He ran up the steps. Soon Paul heard him coming back, but he was not coming fast. He was carrying his little crippled brother. He sat down on the bottom step, then sort of squeezed up against the lame child and pointed to the car.

"There she is, Buddy, just like I told you upstairs. His brother gave it to him for Christmas, and it didn't cost him a cent, and someday I'm gonna give you one just like it; then you can see for yourself all the pretty things in the Christmas windows that I've been trying to tell you about."

Paul got out of the car. "Why don't we start seeing them right now," he said and lifted the little lad on to the front seat of his car. The shining-eyed older brother climbed in beside him and the three of them began a memorable holiday ride.

That Christmas Eve Paul learned what Jesus meant when He said: "It is more blessed to give . . ."

C. Roy Angell

35

A Christmas Gift for the Queen

What would you give your bride for a Christmas present if you were a prince and she the Queen of England. That was a problem Prince Albert had, a hundred and more years ago.

Victoria, Albert's queen bride, already had everything a pretty young lady's heart could wish for — including a golden crown that was studded with diamonds and rubies. For her wedding to the good German prince, the February before, Victoria had received hundreds of fabulous gifts. Prince Albert longed to give his bride something so new and different that her eyes would sparkle and her heart be made glad.

"We're going to have such a wonderful English Christmas, Albert," Victoria said gaily. "You haven't heard our carols and you've never seen the Yule log brought in and set alight with last year's charred one. Why, you've never even tasted English plum pudding!"

"We have happy Yuletide customs in my German homeland too," the Prince replied with a smile. Victoria's words had just given the prince an idea. "Be sure that you stay away from the great ballroom until Christmas Eve; and no spying by your ladies-in-waiting, either!" he told her with a mock frown.

"Oh, a surprise!" Victoria clapped her hands with delight, for even queens love surprises.

For a week before Christmas that year, Buckingham Palace was in a flurry. Everyone in the Empire was especially glad this Christmas because of the happiness of their queen, Victoria. Her marriage to Prince Albert had brought gay laughter to her lips and dancing to her feet. This would be a joyous Yuletide for the people of England, for they loved their queen.

On the day before Christmas the palace was in just the same sort of breathless confusion as your home and mine on that exciting day. Since early morning, Prince Albert, with several pages, had closeted himself in the great ballroom. Victoria, bursting with curiosity, could hear hammering on the other side of the oak doors.

"Can't you give me the tiniest hint?" she later asked Prince Albert.

"Indeed I shan't, my little queen," he teased, adding, "you shall see tonight, when all the court gathers in the great ballroom to drink a cup of wassail to your royal health."

At last, night came. Minstrels with bells on their caps and jackets sang to sweet music of the harp. Pages paraded in, dragging the festive Yule log, all twined with green. When it was time for the feast, the banquet table groaned under the quantities of food it held. There was an enormous boar's head on a golden platter. It was garnished with holly and held an apple between its shining teeth.

Last came the footmen, holding flaming plum puddings high above their heads as they sang an old English carol.

When the singing was over, Prince Albert rose from his chair and whispered to Victoria, "Now it is time for my gift to you — from your prince and from his homeland."

The doors of the great ballroom were thrown open. Before them and the entire court was a glittering wonder never seen before in England. In the middle of the great room, on a table, stood a shining tree. To Victoria it seemed something from a fairy tale — almost too beautiful to be true. Lighted candles glittered in its fragrant branches and twinkled like stars in a velvet sky. And on the tip top of the tree was the figure of an angel with outstreched wings holding a wreath in each hand. "Whatever do you call it?" Victoria asked, as she turned to Albert, her eyes shining.

"It's a Christmas tree, my queen," answered Albert. "In my country, every home from palace to cottage has its Christmas fir. We trim them with beauty and light, to brighten the hearts of children on the birthday of the Christ Child."

Victoria gazed at her first Christmas tree in admiration. Besides the candles on the tree, there were gilded nuts hanging from the branches, balls of delicate glass and paper roses of every colour. "There is a legend that on Christmas night the evergreens of the forest blossom to greet the infant Jesus," the prince explained.

"Do you really like your gift, my dear?" asked Albert.

The queen smiled happily and replied, "England and I have much to thank you for. I have a feeling that before many years, every English home will have its own Christmas tree."

Victoria, we know, was right, for the custom of trimming an evergreen tree has gone far and has spread round the world to gladden hearts on the birthday of the Christ Child.

The Gift of the Magi

One dollar and eighty-seven cents. That was all. And sixty cents of it was in pennies. Pennies saved one and two at a time by bargaining with the grocer and the vegetable man and the butcher. Three times Della counted it. One dollar and eighty-seven cents. And the next day would be Christmas.

There was clearly nothing to do but flop down on the shabby little couch and cry. So Della did it. After she finished her cry and attended to her cheeks with a powder puff, she stood by the window and looked out dully at a grey cat walking a grey fence in a grey backyard. She had only $1.87 with which to buy Jim a present. She had been saving every penny she could with only this sad result. The twenty dollars a week that Jim earned didn't go far. Della had only the $1.87 to buy a present for Jim. Something fine and rare and sterling — something worthy of the honour of being owned by James Dillingham Young. *Her Jim!*

Suddenly she whirled from the window and stood before the mirror. Rapidly she pulled down her hair and let it fall to its full length. Now, there were two possessions of the James Dillingham Youngs in which they both took a mighty pride. One was Jim's gold watch that had been his father's and his grandfather's. The other was Della's hair. Had the Queen of Sheba lived in the next flat, Della's hair would have put to shame Her Majesty's jewels and gifts. Had King Solomon been the janitor, with all his treasures piled up in the basement, Jim would have pulled out his watch every time he passed, knowing that Solomon would turn green with envy.

Nervously and quickly Della once again put up her beautiful hair. On went her old brown jacket; on went her old brown hat. Once she faltered for a minute while a tear splashed on the worn red carpet. Then, with a whirl of skirts, she went out of the door and down the steps to the street.

Where she stopped the sign read: 'Mme. Sofronie, Hair Goods Bought and Sold. All Kinds.' One flight up Della ran and, panting, asked Madame Sofronie, "Will you buy my hair?"

"I buy hair," said Madame. "Take your hat off and let's have a look at it."

Down rippled Della's brown cascade of hair.

"Twenty dollars," said Madame, touching the hair with a practised hand.

"Give it to me quick," said Della.

Oh, how the next two hours tripped by on rosy wings! Della was ransacking the stores for Jim's present and she found it at last. It surely had been made for Jim and no one else. No longer need Jim use a shabby old leather strap for his grand watch. For Della had found a platinum watch-chain, simple and chaste in design. It was even worthy of The Watch. It was like Jim. Quietness and value. Twenty-one dollars it cost and she hurried home with the remaining eighty-seven cents.

When Della reached home she got out her curling-irons and went to work. Within forty minutes her head was covered with tiny close-lying curls that made her look wonderfully like a truant schoolboy. Then she waited for Jim. When she heard Jim's step on the stairs she turned white for just a moment. She had a habit of saying little silent prayers about the simplest everyday things, and now she whispered: "Please, God, make him think I am still pretty."

The door opened and in stepped Della's Jim. He looked thin and very serious. Poor fellow, he was only twenty-two. He needed a new overcoat and he was without gloves.

The minute Jim stepped inside the door, his eyes were fixed upon Della and his expression almost terrified her. It was not anger, not surprise, nor disapproval, nor horror, nor any of the sentiments that she had been prepared for. Jim simply stared with a peculiar expression on his face.

Della gulped her prayer and went to him.

"Jim, darling," she cried, "don't look at me that way. I had my hair cut off and sold it because I couldn't have lived through Christmas without giving you a present. It'll grow out again — you won't mind, will you? I just had to do it. My hair grows awfully fast. Say 'Merry Christmas!' Jim, and let's be happy."

"You've cut off your hair?" asked Jim, laboriously.

"Cut it off and sold it," said Della. "Don't you like me just as well anyhow? I'm me without my hair, ain't I?"

Jim looked about the room curiously.

"You say your hair is gone?" he said, with an air almost of idiocy.

"Please try to understand," pleaded Della. "It's Christmas Eve! Oh Jim, the hairs on my head were numbered, but nobody could ever count my love for you."

Out of his trance Jim seemed to quickly wake. He wrapped his arms around his Della. Then Jim drew a package from his overcoat pocket and threw it upon the table.

"Don't misunderstand, Dell," he said, "I don't think there's anything in the way of a haircut or even a shaved head that could make me like my girl any less. But if you'll unwrap that package you may see why you had me going awhile at first."

Della's fingers tore at the string and paper. And then she let out an ecstatic scream of joy; which quickly changed to hysterical tears and wails. It took all the comforting powers that Jim could bring to bear to quiet her.

For there lay The Combs — the set of combs that Della had worshipped for long in a Broadway window. Beautiful, expensive combs, pure tortoise-shell, with jewelled rims — to wear in the beautiful vanished hair. Even without hope, her heart had simply craved and yearned over them. And now they were hers, but the hair that should have been adorned by the coveted combs was now gone.

But she hugged them to her bosom, then at length she looked up with dim eyes and a smile and said, "My hair grows so fast, Jim!"

And then Della leaped up and cried, "Oh, oh!" for Jim had not yet seen his beautiful present. She held it out to him eagerly. The dull precious metal seemed to flash with a reflection of Della's bright and ardent spirit.

"Isn't it a dandy, Jim? I hunted all over town to find it. You'll have to look at the time a hundred times a day now. Give me your watch — I want to see how it looks on it."

Instead of obeying, Jim tumbled down on the couch and put his hands under the back of his head and smiled.

"Dell," said he, "let's put our Christmas presents away and keep 'em awhile. I sold the watch to buy your combs. And now suppose you put the dinner on!"

The Magi, as you know, were wise men — wonderfully wise men — who brought gifts to the Babe in the manger. They invented the art of giving Christmas presents. Being wise, their gifts were no doubt wise ones. And here is lamely related to you the uneventful chronicle of two foolish children in a poor flat who most unwisely sacrificed for each other their greatest treasures. But in a last word to the wise of these days let it be said that of all who give gifts these two were the wisest. Of all who give and receive gifts, such as they are the wisest. Everywhere they are the wisest. They are the Magi.

Adapted and abridged from the story by O. Henry

The Yule Log and the Holy Babe

The snow lay deep around the castle walls one Christmas Eve in England long ago. Inside, the huge Yule Log, laid upon the hearth and kindled from the charred remains of last year's Log, burst into flame. As if in gratitude for the warmth and light, the voices of all who gathered in the great hall were raised in song:

> Welcome be Thou, Heavenly King, Welcome — born on this morning.
> Welcome, Thou for whom we sing — Welcome Yule!

Stung by the icy wind and suffering with pangs of hunger, five-year-old Catherine and her family struggled through the last deep snowdrifts. Soon they would enter the castle gate to gather with the other tenant farmers and their families.

Pressed tightly to her heart, in small hands numb with cold, Catherine carried a crudely carved figure of the Baby Jesus, a precious gift from her father, and given to her on this very Christmas Eve. Deeply moved by her father's stories of the Holy Birth, she recalled the helplessness of the Baby Jesus — His hunger — His cold in the dampness of the stable grotto. Now, one desire crowded all else from Catherine's soul — to protect the Holy Babe — to keep Him warm!

At last they reached the great castle hall and joined with the others. How warm and inviting the huge Yule Log seemed to all. Hope rose in each heart as the flames leaped and danced. The winter frost had come early and this year's harvest had been poor. The tenant farmers and their families were close to starvation. But now — and for as long as the Yule Log burned — they would be fed, for by tradition and law, until the flames of the Yule Log died, even an unwilling Lord of the Castle must feed and shelter his tenants and their families.

Suddenly the side doors opened wide to the sound of trumpets. The great feast in honour of the birthday of Jesus Christ had begun. All eyes were instantly fastened on the trays of food carried in by servants. All hands were poised, ready to pile high their plates with food, to fill to overflowing their cups, as the trays of meat and drink were placed on the tables around the hall.

But little Catherine, even though hungry, was still wrapped in her one desire; to protect her image of the Holy Babe. Acutely aware of the cold in the drafty old hall, Catherine made her way to the great hearth and huddled as close to the Yule Log as she dared. Catherine drew forth the small wooden figure of the Holy Babe, tenderly crooning a lullaby as she cradled and rocked Him in her arms until she was sure He was warm. Although Catherine had no manger in which to lay the sweet Baby Jesus and no warm blanket of straw with which to cover Him, she found a protected chink in the stone wall of the fireplace surrounding the hearth. Lovingly she placed the figure of the Babe there and gave a deep sigh of relief, knowing that the Yule Log would keep Him cosy and warm. Quickly, Catherine slipped back to the long table and joined her parents and brothers who were enjoying their long-awaited meal.

Soon afterwards, Catherine, well fed and warmed, drifted into sleep amid sounds of laughter and joy. Vividly she dreamed! She dreamed that the carved wooden Babe had come to life and, reaching out His small hand, caressed her cheek as He blessed all who were gathered in the great hall.

Almost as a miracle, the Yule Log continued to burn for many days and nights and a sense of strange wonder awoke in those who were sheltered in the castle. But little Catherine did not wonder. Her dream of the Holy Babe, reaching out to everyone, was vivid and fresh in her mind. She was sure it was His blessing which kept the Yule Log burning and which warmed each heart. Perhaps Catherine was right — for even the great Lord of the Castle felt a strange new glow of compassion and love enter his heart. And before the embers of the Yule Log died out, he met with his tenants in the great hall and promised that food and firewood from his own stores would be shared with all until the sun-warmed earth could yield its fruits once more.

Watch Out for That Donkey!

Legends and stories from the earliest years of Christianity tell us of the roles played so lovingly by animals in the Holy Birth; but here's a story about one animal who was *not* so loving!

"Watch out for that donkey — he's mean!" warned the innkeeper's wife as she left Mary and Joseph in the humble shelter of the stable-grotto and hurried back to her work in the crowded inn.

Assa, the small brown donkey, eyed, with suspicion, the two humans making themselves comfortable in *his* home, the cave which he grudgingly shared with old Kina, the cow. Used to biting and kicking his way through life, the little donkey was surprised by the gentle, smiling look the lady gave him — a look which said she understood that life had never been very good to him either! Assa was even more surprised when the man brought fresh hay and laid it before both the donkey and the cow.

But during the night, things became just too much for the donkey! A baby was born to the humans in his cave! Now that baby was asleep in *his* manger! The man and the woman were dozing and the old cow was staring adoringly at the sleeping child. It was just too much! No one was paying the least bit of attention to Assa! So great was his annoyance that at last he let forth a great raucous bray. The man jumped up and the baby cried. The little donkey was delighted! Perhaps he would be beaten but he was certainly noticed! He started to bray again but the lady, roused from sleep, sat up and looked right into his eyes. Gently, in a lullaby whisper, she spoke to him, "Hush-sh-sh, dear donkey. My little one must sleep."

No human had ever spoken to him that way before and no sound or bray would come forth from his throat. For long hours afterward, the donkey remembered the sound of the lady's voice and felt a strange peace and warmth. But, once again, rebellion triumphed in the stubborn little donkey. He felt hungry — and there in the manger, around the baby, were the choicest morsels of soft, clean hay! Stealthily the donkey made his way to the manger. Greedily he began to nibble at the hay around the sleeping babe. Suddenly he stopped! The baby had opened its eyes and, reaching out his little hand, took hold of the donkey's soft, furry ear. With a look of delight, the baby smiled at the donkey — a smile of love that went right into the heart of the rebellious donkey like warm sunshine. Years of mean, stubborn anger melted away — all painful memories of loads that were too heavy, of curses and beatings, were no more.

And when Mary and Joseph awoke near dawn, they found a now peaceful little donkey *kneeling* by the manger while the sleeping Baby Jesus clasped in His tiny hand the donkey's soft, furry ear.

From St. Nicholas to Santa Claus and Father Christmas

The 'Spirit of Giving' has always been a part of Christmas. The very first people to hear of the Holy Birth, the shepherds, were inspired to bring tokens of their love and joy to the Christ Child. The Gospels also tell about the Three Wise Men who came bearing gifts to the Holy Babe.

In every age and in every land, the Spirit of Giving shows itself in many special forms and each in a different dress. In Sweden, it is the delightful little elf, the Yul Tomten, who delivers gifts in a sleigh drawn by goats of the Thunder God, Thor. Yul Tomten wears a red suit and cap, very similar to that worn by Santa Claus and Father Christmas. Denmark has its Julmanden, who is carried by reindeer, and Norway has the Julsvenn. In Italy it is La Befana, an old woman, who brings the gifts. In Spain and in all Spanish-speaking countries, the Spirit of Giving rides as the Three Kings.

Several countries in Europe and Africa have a Father Christmas; and in parts of Switzerland there is a Mother Christmas who travels with him as well! Luckily for us, there is a real world traveller, good St. Nicholas who, after he arrived in America, soon became Santa Claus — who in turn, travelled back across the ocean to merry England and met old Father Christmas. And this is their story!

About three hundred years after Jesus lived, a boy was born in a far away country. His name was Nicholas and from early childhood he showed, in many ways, that he loved God. When he grew to manhood and became a bishop, he used the great wealth that God had given him to help others. Now, Nicholas didn't want anyone to know of his loving deeds, but once he was discovered as he quietly left his gift in the middle of the night.

Nicholas had so much of the Spirit of Giving in him that his fame soon spread all over Europe. Bishop Nicholas became St. Nicholas, and many stories and legends tell us of his generosity to all people — and especially to children. Even today, children in other countries eagerly await his coming on December 6, St. Nicholas' Day, when he brings his gifts.

The people of Holland long ago adopted St. Nicholas as their Spirit of Giving; and after the Dutch settled in America, they asked St. Nicholas to visit them in their new homeland. For you see, their children were very lonely without him.

In New Amsterdam, which later became New York, pictures of the tall, lean saint in his high hat and long red bishop's robe were seen all over the city. The children's pet name for St. Nicholas was Sinter Klaus.

Many of the English families who had also settled in America were Puritans and their religion did not allow them to celebrate Christmas. During Cromwell's Puritan rule in England, all celebration of Christmas had been banned, and with it Britain's boisterous old Father Christmas.

After a time, however, some English children in America noticed that Sinter Klaus always brought gifts to their Dutch neighbours. They asked that Sinter Klaus, or 'Santa Claus' as they pronounced it, would visit them too! And, as he loves all children, Santa Claus soon filled English stockings as well as Dutch wooden shoes.

As more families from Scandinavia, Germany, and from all over Europe settled in America, the Christmas customs they had brought from their homelands began to blend. The settlers became more Americanised as changing times affected speech, dress, and transportation. These same changes affected St. Nicholas — or Santa Claus. His tall pointed bishop's hat, although still pointed, no longer stood up straight, and a white furry tassel was fastened on the end. St. Nicholas' red bishop's robe became a red fitted suit, trimmed with white fur — and as Santa Claus he gained a great deal of weight and became jollier and jollier! In America he began to travel by reindeer-sled, instead of by horseback as in Holland.

Meanwhile, in England, what had happened to Father Christmas? Well, this vigorous, jolly old party-goer, so familiar to all Englishmen from the old English Mummers' plays, was becoming popular once again. Still crowned with holly and dressed in a loose red robe and full red hood, he was busy bringing back the spirit of merrymaking to English Christmas celebrations. Although less boisterous than before Cromwell's time, Father Christmas still represented only fun and pleasure — but now all that was to change.

No one is quite certain when Santa's reindeer-drawn sleigh carried him across the Atlantic Ocean to England, but every English child knows that he made the trip! There, Santa Claus met with Britain's ancient, merry-making Father Christmas. And strange as it may seem, from that time on, Father Christmas began to mellow — to grow more compassionate — and even to look different. Gradually, his crown of holly fell away and his loose red robe and hood disappeared. Some say that Santa may even have introduced Father Christmas to his own tailor, for they soon began to dress exactly alike! In fact, there are many who now ask: "Are they really *two* jolly old saints looking like identical twins, who love to keep us guessing — or have Father Christmas and Santa Claus become one and the same?"

The wise ones say that the Spirit of Giving still shows himself in many ways. And whether he is called Père Noel as in France, Weihnachtsmann as in Germany, Sinter Claus, Santa Claus or Father Christmas, he is still the same Spirit of Giving, who excites the hearts of children everywhere. And with each toy and present that he leaves, he gives a part of himself — a gift that he hopes we will keep forever — the Spirit of Giving.

43

Christmastide

The Christmas Story

According to the Gospel of Matthew

Now when Jesus was born in Bethlehem of Judaea in the days of Herod the king, behold, there came wise men from the east to Jerusalem, saying, Where is he that is born King of the Jews? for we have seen his star in the east, and are come to worship him."

When Herod the king had heard *these things,* he was troubled, and all Jerusalem with him. And when he had gathered all the chief priests and scribes of the people together, he demanded of them where Christ should be born. And they said unto him, In Bethlehem of Judaea: for thus it is written by the prophet, And thou Bethlehem, *in* the land of Judah, are not the least among the princes of Judah: for out of thee shall come a Governor, that shall rule my people Israel.

Then Herod, when he had privily called the wise men, inquired of them diligently what time the star appeared. And he sent them to Bethlehem, and said, Go and search diligently for the young child; and when ye have found *him,* bring me word again, that I may come and worship him also.

When they had heard the king, they departed; and lo, the star, which they saw in the east, went before them, till it came and stood over where the young child was. When they saw the star, they rejoiced with exceeding great joy.

And when they were come into the house, they saw the young child with Mary his mother, and fell down, and worshipped him: and when they had opened their treasures, they presented unto him gifts; gold, and frankincense, and myrrh.

Matthew 2:1-11

44

The Gifts of the Three Wise Men

The hearts of the Three Wise Men were troubled. What had happened? They could no longer see the star which they had followed for so many miles and days. Must they return to their homes without finding the Holy Child?

The Three Wise Men were Magi, followers of an ancient Persian teacher. They knew the prophecies which foretold the birth of God's own Son on earth and they were wise in understanding what the stars foretold about happenings on earth. Melchior, old Balthazar and young Caspar, who came from Africa, were learned in mathematics, in astronomy and in medicine — in short, they were masters of all the wisdom that men and women had gained on earth since earliest times.

All three of the Wise Men were 'Kings' because each had an extra special power. In Melchior's wise presence, people became wiser; through

Balthazar's great compassion, people's sorrows lightened and through Caspar's power to heal, the bodies of many men, women and children were strengthened.

Yet, even with all their knowledge and compassion, the Three Kings felt that they had been living in a dark world. How they yearned for the Child, the Everlasting King of Light, to be born upon the earth! Then, at last, the sign of His birth had come — a Star more brilliant than any in the heavens.

But as they followed the Star and neared the city of Jerusalem, where the wicked King Herod ruled, a dark cloud came between the Three Wise Men and the Star. Anxiously they asked everyone they met, "Where can we find the Child who will be the King of the Jews?"

When King Herod learned that Wise Men were seeking a newborn King of the Jews he became enraged. The birth of a rival King terrified him!

45

Herod called together his chief priests and scribes and asked them where this Child was to be born. "The old prophecies tell that He will be born in Bethlehem," they told him. Herod sent for the Wise Men. Cunningly he charmed them: "When you have found the Child, come back and tell me where He is so that I, too, may worship Him."

As the Three Kings travelled the winding road from Jerusalem to Bethlehem, legend tells that the dark cloud still hid the light of the Star until they reached an ancient well and stopped to drink. Suddenly, as they gazed into its crystal clear water, their eyes were dazzled — for there in the water was the brilliant reflection of the Star!

Joyfully, the Three Kings mounted their camels. Once more they followed the Star into the town and through the narrow streets of Bethlehem until they saw the Star hovering over a certain house. They entered and there they found the Christ Child, asleep in Mary's arms. Reverently the Wise Men, in their kingly garb, sank to their knees to adore Him. One by one, in the name of all mankind, they presented their gifts to the sleeping Child.

"Oh, Holy Child," prayed Melchior, "You who will bring the golden light of heavenly wisdom into the thoughts of men and women — accept my offering of gold!"

"Oh, Holy Child," prayed Balthazar, "You who will bring to earth the true power to love unselfishly — accept the gift of frankincense."

"Oh, Holy Child," prayed Caspar, "You who will someday save mankind from the forces of death and grant to men of good will your power to heal — accept the gift of myrrh."

For a moment all was peaceful and quiet in the soft glow of the oil lamps within the small room. Then, slowly, the tiny Baby stirred and opened His eyes. One of His little hands gently rose and a blissful smile played upon His sweet lips. Gradually the room became filled with light — light more brilliant than that of the guiding Star. The Three Wise Men knew that their gifts had been accepted.

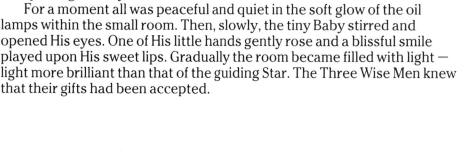

The Twelve Days of Christmastide

The Advent waiting now is done
And Mary has her little Son;
For Him our hearts are open wide —
And so begins the Christmastide!
For twelve more days — each Holy Night —
His Star and Angels bring us light.

Now Gifts and Treasures they'll reveal
If in some quiet times we kneel,
Remembering — 'mid season's joy —
Why Wise Men sought that Holy Boy.
Then bless'd will be our Christmastide
Through which the Wise Three Kings still ride.

When Christianity became the religion of the Roman Empire the days between December 25 and January 6 became known as the Twelve Holy Days. The northern Germanic peoples figure their calendars by nights rather than by days and so for them, the Holy Days became the 'Holy Nights.' These days and nights also bear the name of Christmastide.*

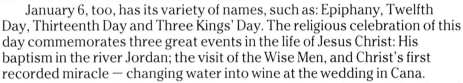

January 6, too, has its variety of names, such as: Epiphany, Twelfth Day, Thirteenth Day and Three Kings' Day. The religious celebration of this day commemorates three great events in the life of Jesus Christ: His baptism in the river Jordan; the visit of the Wise Men, and Christ's first recorded miracle — changing water into wine at the wedding in Cana.

The Christian Festival of Epiphany is even older than the celebration of Christmas! 'Epiphany' means 'manifestation' or 'appearance' and originally this day celebrated the Baptism of Jesus. It was then that John the Baptist saw the Spirit of God descending like a dove upon Jesus and heard the voice of God saying, "This is my Beloved Son."** Thus, during the Baptism, God became *manifest* in Jesus Christ.

Since the fifth century, however, the celebration of Epiphany in Western Christian churches† stresses the Visit of the Wise Men to the Christ Child. To them it was *manifested* that the Saviour of mankind had been born.

In some lands this festive day is popularly called Three Kings' Day. Throughout the ages these stately Wise Men have captured the imagination of young and old alike. Even today, in many lands, people crowd the streets to watch colourful pageants and parades in which the Three Kings ride. In most Spanish-speaking countries it is at Three Kings' time, rather than at Christmas, that children receive their gifts. The gift bringers are the Three Kings themselves.

In other countries, children form small groups and walk through their neighbourhoods or villages on the eve of Three Kings' Day. Each group is led by a child who carries a star at the end of a pole. Often the 'star followers' are dressed to represent the Three Kings.

The Bible tells us little about the Three Kings. It does not tell us that they were 'Kings' or 'Magi' or even how many came to worship the Holy Child. We are told only that "there came wise men from the east". Yet church traditions, as well as legends and stories about the Three Kings, are rich with images which speak to our hearts.

* On various traditional church calendars Christmastide includes St. Stephen's Day (Boxing Day) — December 26; the day of St. John the Evangelist — December 27; Holy Innocents Day — December 28; New Year's Eve 'Night Watch' — December 31; Holy Name Day (New Year's Day) — January 1.

** Matthew 3:16, 17 — Mark 1:10, 11 — Luke 3:22

† Roman Catholic and Protestant churches, as distinct from the Greek Orthodox, Russian Orthodox and other Eastern churches.

Boxing Day

December 26

In Great Britain, Canada and Australia December 26 is called Boxing Day. The name 'Boxing' dates from the Middle Ages when it was customary to open the church 'poor box' on this day and share the money among the poor. Another 'Boxing' custom was presenting money as a gift, in a small box, to those who had given service during the year, such as the postman, the milkman and the servants.

In modern Boxing Day observances, many families attend theatres and modern versions of the age-old 'Christmas Pantomimes', in which traditional stories are mixed with dancing and light-hearted fun. Sports and outdoor activities are a welcome change after the heavy eating and celebrations of Christmas. City parks are crowded with children and their model aeroplanes, roller skates and bicycles. In Canada and wherever there is plenty of snow, sledging, building snowmen and snowball contests are a common sight. In Australia, where the season is summer, swimming, surfing and yacht-racing mark Boxing Day.

In the United States, December 26 is not observed as a holiday nor known as 'Boxing Day'. However, it is a day when gifts which 'do not fit' are 'boxed' and returned to stores or exchanged.

In many Christian countries December 26 is also celebrated as St. Stephen's Day, and it is a good time for taking stock of what Christmas has meant to each of us personally; and to look ahead and think of good things we hope to accomplish in the New Year.

The Feast of Stephen

December 26

The Feast of Stephen, celebrated on December 26, was once an important religious holiday. The day after the birth of Jesus was especially chosen to honour Stephen because the Bible tells us he was willing to give his life for his belief in Jesus Christ as the Son of God. He became the first Christian martyr.*

One of our favourite carols tells of a legendary deed of kindness performed on this day by 'Good King Wenceslas'.

> Good King Wenceslas looked out,
> On the feast of Stephen,
> When the snow lay round about,
> Deep and crisp and even.

This beautiful carol goes on to tell how Wenceslas and his page braved the 'winter's rage' to take food, wine and firewood to a poor peasant.

History tells us that Wenceslas, the Duke of Bohemia, lived in the tenth century and that he helped spread Christianity over much of what is now Czechoslovakia. He was deeply loved by his people and to them he was 'Good *King* Wenceslas' for he ruled with both wisdom and kindness.

* The Acts of the Apostles 6-7

The Gift Bringers

While our Santa Claus, St. Nicholas or Father Christmas rest by a warm fire, other Gift Bringers around the world prepare for their busiest time on Three Kings' Day.

Soon the Three Kings will ride again in many countries throughout Europe and Central and South America, bringing gifts to sleeping children. But before they go to sleep, the children will leave hay or grass for the Three Kings' horses or camels. And it is a camel, the 'lit'lest' camel, who is the gift-bringer for Christian children in the Middle East.

The Lit'lest Camel

The Three Kings rode by night and day
To reach the place where Jesus lay,
And though the Three Kings were inspired,
Alas, their camels just grew tired —
Especially the lit'lest one,
Who grew so weak he couldn't run.
He ached from camel hump to knee —
This was his first long trip, you see.
Yet he had heard the Three Kings say
That through the Christ Child's love, someday,
All hatred, strife and war would cease,
And lion and lamb would dwell in peace.

So though he wasn't very strong,
The lit'lest camel struggled on,
And all his pain he bravely bore
Until they reached the Christ Child's door.
But having done his job so well,
Exhausted, the small camel fell.
The Christ Child came and blessed him then
For helping bring the Three Wise Men;
And promised that for what he'd done,
Each Three Kings' Day he'd have the fun
Of bringing gifts to girls and boys —
Some sweets, a doll or little toys.

Now, Christian children, all aglow,
Await His coming and they know
The lit'lest camel never tires!
He brings them all their hearts' desires.

49

Midwinter Night's Dream

Christopher was lost. There was no doubt about that. And all because he'd been daydreaming about elves! Now the snowfall was growing heavy and soon it would be dark!

It was Christmas Day and Chris knew his parents would be worried. "How could you be so dumb as to get lost?" he asked himself irritably. "You just weren't paying attention to where you were going!"

And that was certainly true, for Chris had been busy thinking of the talk he'd had with his grandmother about elves — and fairies and gnomes! Christopher, in his heart, felt sure that elves were real, but the other children at his school in the valley laughed at the idea. So did his teachers! On the other hand, the villagers who lived in the mountains said, "Of course there are elves, any fool knows that!" And Grandmother, who as far as Chris was concerned knew almost everything, said, "Listen, Chris, God's world is filled with 'invisibles'. There are Angels to do God's work, why not elves and gnomes and a whole host of fairy beings that work for Him in nature?"

A moment later, without warning, the snow-covered earth gave way beneath his feet. Down Chris tumbled, rolling over and over until he landed with a thud against the wall of a small underground cavern.

Chris lay very still, dazed and shaken.

Suddenly a small shrill voice commanded, "Wake up! Wake up, lazy bones!"

Unable to tell if he was awake or dreaming, Chris looked up to find a wizened, white-bearded dwarf, about half a metre tall, holding a lantern and peering into his face.

"W-who are you?" Chris stammered.

"Humph!" said the little dwarf. "You may call me 'Mister Gnome'. And you're to come with me. She wants to see you!"

"Excuse me, sir," replied Chris politely, "but I can't go with you. I don't even know who She is."

"Why, She who lives under the mountains and meadows and seas!" said Mister Gnome, as if that explained everything. "Oh, wait here!" he commanded, and with that he whirled round and before Christopher's astonished eyes, disappeared — right into the rock wall.

A moment later, with a sudden 'pop', the little gnome's head appeared from out of the rock. Just his head! With an almost comical attempt at dignity he reported, "She says that I am to say 'Please come with me'. You will be quite safe."

"I really must be dreaming," Chris thought. So quite cheerfully he said, "All right, Mister Gnome."

Pop, pop, bing, ping, pop! Suddenly from everywhere, out of the stone walls somersaulted dozens of small luminous lights which, before Christopher's amazed eyes, shaped themselves into fully formed gnomes and elves. They were not all alike. Oh, no! They were many different shapes and sizes and colours. Quickly they gathered around Christopher and studied him with great curiosity as they formed themselves into a kind of living travelling seat.

"Climb on. We'll carry you to She who lives under the mountains and meadows and seas," said one friendly little red elf.

"But I can't go through the earth as you do!" cried Christopher in dismay. "Your wide-awake, hard-body can't," explained the red elf, "but your dream-body can."

Christopher sat himself on the gnome-made travelling couch and in a twinkle, without even a bump, he was carried right through the stone wall.

Faster and faster Christopher travelled on his living magic carpet. Through tunnels and caverns where gold and precious jewels glittered and shimmered. Then, with startling suddeness, Chris found himself in a huge hollow chamber filled with misty light and colour.

He heard the most beautiful music, and the loveliest voice whispered, "Welcome, Christopher."

From the mist a beautiful face began to form and She spoke again, "I have watched you, Chris, walking in my mountains. I've seen your love for my trees and flowers, my stones and my brooks. Do you know who I am?"

"You m-must be 'Mother Earth'," the boy answered with a gulp.

She smiled. "You're right. I want you to see what happens beneath my soil on these special winter nights, Chris. I want you to take that message to other children in the outer world."

Soon, Christopher, on his magic cloud of gnomes and elves, was shown fields of sleeping seeds, lying just below the surface of the earth. And within each seed he saw the glow of a tiny speck of life.

"Each seed is dreaming now, Chris, of the tree or plant it will become," said Mother Earth.

But Christopher was too astonished to answer for he saw that everywhere there were gnomes and elves, weaving around the seeds, like tiny nursemaids. They smoothed and softened each seed-bed. They brought elf-broth to feed the seeds and rayed out warmth to keep their tiny charges from becoming too cold.

Filled with joy at the beauty of what he saw, Chris cried out, "Oh, how wonderful! How beautiful you are!" And as they heard his words all the gnomes and elves began to sing a kind of melody.

"You see, Chris," said Mother Earth, "when humans praise them they can sing with joy and their work becomes easier. Tell the other children, Christopher. Many will laugh at you, but be brave. Tell them that their earth is a living earth. Ask them to love and protect me. I need their help.

"And now, farewell. Remember, tell the children . . . tell the children . . . tell the children . . . tell the children . . ."

Mother Earth's voice grew more and more distant as Christopher felt his dream-body being carried back to the small cave into which he had fallen, back his now wide-awake body.

Christopher sat up and rubbed his eyes. Daylight was sifting into the cave. The snowstorm was over.

Cautiously the boy climbed out the cave and looked around at the snow-white world. Suddenly his heart skipped a beat, for there in the valley, not far below, was his village. "Thank you, God, for keeping me safe," he said aloud.

Then Christopher turned and looked down into the darkness of the small cave. "Good-bye, Mister Gnome. Good-bye, little red elf," he whispered. "Good-bye, Mother Earth. Perhaps it was only in a dream that I met you, but for me you will always be alive and real."

The Flight to Egypt

The clouds of fear and hatred that surrounded King Herod grew thicker after his visit with the Wise Men. God's Angels watched and observed, "Herod is afraid that the Christ Child will become King in his place. He will try to kill the Child."

"Yes," said the Archangel Michael, "it will be a sad and terrible time in Bethlehem. Many innocent souls will soon be coming from earth into our special care, for Herod will send soldiers to kill all the boy children in Bethlehem under the age of two. The Holy Child must leave Bethlehem."

"I will go to Joseph and warn him," said the Archangel Gabriel. "Joseph often asks the blessings of the Angels and he will hear me. The Wise Men, too, will heed my warning when I tell them they must not return to tell Herod they have found the Child."

Later, after the Three Wise Men had left their precious gifts of gold, frankincense and myrrh by the cradle of the sleeping Christ Child, they heard the warning of the Angel. At once they left the land of Israel in secret and returned to their own lands.

Joseph, too, in a dream, heard the warning of the Angel; and under the blanket of darkness he fled from Bethlehem with Mary and the Babe. And so it came to pass that when Herod sent his guards to destroy all the baby boys in Bethlehem, the Christ Child was no longer there.

The Legend of the Donkey

After the Angel's warning, Mary and Joseph had travelled many miles. Mary, holding the baby Jesus in her arms, rode upon a donkey while Joseph walked by their side. The only sound to break the silence was the little donkey's slow, rhythmic clip-clop, clip-clop. How drowsy Mary was! How weary Joseph felt! At last Joseph led the little donkey to a sheltered

spot some distance from the caravan road. He lit a small fire and made a bed of brush for Mary and the Child. Mary's sweet voice crooned a lullaby for Jesus. Then they all drifted into sleep.

Only the little donkey heard the distant sounds of Herod's guards who were searching for the Holy Child. Joseph's fire, still burning, was visible as it cast its orange glow into the darkness. The donkey tried to awaken and warn the family but could not for he had only a gentle neigh, and they did not hear him. Closer and closer came the sounds of Herod's guards. More and more agitated grew the little donkey — until at last, with a great effort, he gave a strong, piercing bray. Joseph awoke and saw their danger. Quickly he put out the fire, so that when Herod's guards came close, they passed by in the darkness. The family was safe.

And to this day, the donkey's piercing bray is a reminder of his service and devotion to the little Christ Child and His family.

The Legend of the Rosemary

In the morning after they awoke, Mary and Joseph discovered a small stream and knelt to give thanks to the Heavenly Father for His protecting care; for the donkey who had warned and saved them; for the sun which gave them light; for the sheltering darkness which hid them from sight; and now, for the stream which gave its sweet water for them to drink.

Then Mary washed the Baby's little clothes in the small stream and hung them on a bush to dry. In the warmth of the sun the bush gave forth a

delightful fragrance, and when the Baby's clothes were dry they carried the fragrance of the plant.

"How lovely," whispered Mary, "bless you, little plant, for your scented gift. I shall think of you forever as Mary's rose." As Mary smiled, suddenly the Baby Jesus reached out His hand and touched the plant. At once, tiny blue flowers sprang forth upon the bush — the same colour of heavenly blue as Mary's robe. And ever since, the fragrant little plant has been known as Rosemary.

The Legend of the Wheat Field

It was a long and difficult journey from Bethlehem to Egypt. Wherever they could, Mary and Joseph avoided the main caravan road where Herod's guards might easily find them. Once they stopped to rest by the side of a ploughed field where a farmer was sowing his wheat. The farmer greeted them kindly and offered to share his jug of water. As he looked at the Baby Jesus he seemed to hear the Child speak, "Ready your ox and wagon, for your grain will ripen and be fully grown within the day."

The farmer fell to his knees. "Why you must be our blessed Messiah, our Saviour," he exclaimed. "At last you have been born!"

The Christ Child smiled. His lips did not move but the farmer clearly heard Him say, "You shall be blessed because you have recognised me. Tomorrow guards will come seeking for us. Do not be afraid to tell them the truth — that a man, a woman and a child passed by when your wheat was being sown."

Next day, as the farmer was reaping the ripe grain which had grown overnight, Herod's guards appeared. Their Captain demanded to know if a man, a woman and a child had passed that way.

"Oh yes," replied the farmer, truthfully, "when I was sowing my wheat."

"The ones we seek did not pass this way," said the Captain to his guards, "for this ripe wheat had to be sown weeks ago." And so the guards turned aside and sought another road.

The Legends of On

The mighty wisdom that lived in very early Egypt had almost disappeared. Only a few holy men of Egypt remained; sage-priests who lived quietly, almost hidden away, near the ruins of the old temple of Heliopolis — or On, as the Bible calls it.

Near that same temple lived a community of very religious Jews who worked as gardeners for wealthy Egyptian merchants and nobles. And, say the legends, it was to this place in Egypt that Joseph brought Mary and the Holy Babe.

Today, the On of the Bible still exists. It is a simple Egyptian village and near its centre, in the courtyard of a small church, is a tree that is more than two thousand years old. It is called 'Mary's tree'.

And — so the legends tell — in the shadow of the ruins of the once great temple of On, in the midst of a community of learned and pious men who loved the God of Israel, Jesus spent his first years.

The Bible tells that Jesus remained in Egypt until the death of King Herod so that an old Hebrew prophecy might be fulfilled: "Out of Egypt have I called my son."* Then an Angel of the Lord spoke once more to Joseph in a dream, "Arise and take the young child and His mother and go to the land of Israel."

So Mary, Joseph and Jesus came once more to their own land — but they did not return to Judaea. Taking a different road they went to Nazareth in Galilee, where they made their home for many years.

*Matthew 2:15

And God Send You a Happy New Year!

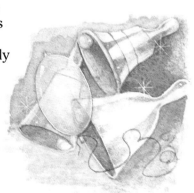

Ring out the old, ring in the new . . .
Ring out the false, ring in the true.*

"Happy New Year! Bonne Année! !Feliz año Nuevo! Felice Anno
Nuovo! Nor Gott Ny År! Viel Glück im Neuen Jahr!"

The custom of beginning the year on January 1 started during Roman
times. The Romans also had a god with two faces who watched the Old
Year go out and the New Year come in. He was called the 'two-faced Janus.'
Our first month, January, is named after him. Another familiar picture from
ancient Rome is Old Father Time, accompanied by the New Year's Babe.

Even though New Year's Day has not been a significant Christian Holy-
day, 'Watch Night' services are held on New Year's Eve. And on New Year's
Day in some churches, Bible passages are read which recall the public
'naming' of the Baby Jesus, eight days after His birth.

'A good beginning makes a good ending' — so starting the year in a
happy frame of mind is all important. In Scotland, New Year's Day and the
day before are known as 'daft days', or 'crazy days' and children joyfully go
from door to door crying "Hogmanay!" No one is quite sure what this
strange word means, but the children know that shouting it
gets them handouts of special oat cakes and cheese.

The world-wide custom of making noise at the start of the year goes
back to really ancient times. Of course, no one ever wanted to start the
year with any evil spirits around, so a fearful din was set up to drive them
away. Today, 'noise makers', clackers, toy trumpets, whistles and bells are
still given as party favours at New Year's Eve celebrations.

In England, the chimes of London's Big Ben announce the arrival of the
New Year as crowds of people stand ready to celebrate in Trafalgar Square
and Piccadilly Circus. It's almost the same in New York's Times Square
where nearly a million people wait and watch for that magic midnight
moment when a giant, brightly coloured electric 'apple' is lowered to the
ground from a tall skyscraper. Then, shouts of "Happy New Year" ring out
and are heard across the country on radio and television.

On New Year's Day in the United States millions of people watch
championship football games in stadiums or on television. In the city of
Philadelphia, Pennsylvania, people jam the streets to watch the famous
Mummers' Parade in which gaily costumed Mummers, wearing enormous
head-dresses, march and dance to merry music. Mummers' parades and
plays were once a common sight in Britain, where they originated, and can
still be found in some towns and villages.

Perhaps the most famous New Year's custom is the making of New
Year's Resolutions. Although many people find that their resolutions are
often broken, just making up the list of changes we want has a value of its
own.

What bright New Years we could all have if every Christian would truly
look for ways to:

Ring out the darkness of the land;
Ring in the Christ that is to be.*

*From 'In Memoriam' by Alfred, Lord Tennyson

Twelfth Night

"On the First Day of Christmas, my true love sent to me, a partridge in a pear tree . . ." and right on through Twelfth Night — as the old carol tells, the gifts kept rolling in ". . . two turtle doves, three French hens, four calling birds, five golden rings, six geese a-laying, seven swans a-swimming, eight maids a-milking, nine ladies dancing, ten lords a-leaping, eleven pipers piping, twelve drummers drumming" along with that one partridge in the pear tree!

During earlier times in England, the Christmas celebrations continued for a full twelve days with the merriest party of all on Twelfth Night, the Eve of Epiphany. Work on the farms only began again on the following 'Plough Monday', when spring ploughing started. Throughout England, in the countryside and in the cities, Twelfth Night was celebrated with song and dance; with 'lords a-leaping' and 'ladies dancing' and with partridges, ducks and geese on the dining tables. Sometimes a Twelfth Night King or Queen was chosen. Some families celebrated with a 'Twelfth Cake'. The lucky boy and girl who found the dried bean and dried pea hidden inside it were crowned King and Queen for the night.

Here We Come A-Wassailing!

Toasting out the Yule Season by drinking to the health of loved ones or friends is a worldwide custom. One of the most colourful of toasting ceremonies is drinking from the old English Wassail Bowl. 'Wassail' comes from the Old Norse 'ves weill', meaning, 'be in health'. Although there are many recipes for Wassail it is basically hot spiced ale or cider containing roasted apples. In olden times in villages throughout Britain, a large Wassail Bowl was 'carried round' during the holidays up until Twelfth Day. The villagers even carried their own cups for sampling! There is also an old custom of pouring Wassail around the roots of an apple tree. A shot-gun is then fired through the branches of the tree while a Wassail song is sung. This ceremony is performed in the hope that the apple trees will be especially fruitful during the forthcoming year. A favourite carol tells of this custom:

> O here we come A-Wassailing, among the leaves so green;
> And here we come A-Wandering, so fair to be seen.
> Love and joy come to you, and to you your Wassail too,
> And God bless you and send you a Happy New Year,
> And God send you a Happy New Year!

What the Three Kings Brought

"This is a personal Christmas story —" writes the now-famous American author, Ruth Sawyer, telling of a memorable event many years ago during her year's visit to Spain.

"It was five days before Twelfth Night or Epiphany — the time when the Three Kings still ride from the East," Miss Sawyer tells us. At that time she was visiting the city of Seville in Spain, seeking old Spanish legends and stories of the *Noche Buena* and *Navidad* — the Good Night and Christmas.

One cold winter morning as she passed through Seville's Parque Maria Luisa she again met Alfredo, the gentle old man who took care of the park. With him on this day was a scrawny, ill-fed, thinly dressed little boy with eyes that seemed too large for his face.

"This is Pepe, *Señora*," Alfredo said, "he has come a long way from a farm in the uplands. He hopes to earn enough money selling seeds to buy a burro for his papa."

With fingers that were blue with cold, the boy held out several packets of seeds to Miss Sawyer. "To feed the birds in the park, *Señora*," he said. "They need much food."

Touched by the child's frail appearance and his obvious courage and simple dignity, Ruth Sawyer responded at once. "I will buy ten packets every day."

The boy's large eyes brightened. "Thank you, *Señora*."

As the money and the packets changed hands, Miss Sawyer, with a warm smile, asked, "Will you tell me more about yourself, Pepe, and about your family?"

The thin, pinched little face lit up and love shone from his eyes as he spoke. "Oh, yes, I want you to know, *Señora*, that my *papacito* is a very good farmer! But now he is sick and there are many mouths to feed. Since the autobus ran over our burro there are many heavy loads to carry. This the *papacito* must not do! So I have come to Seville, and with my seeds I will earn money to buy a young, strong burro to help make him well again, my *papacito*."

Miss Sawyer felt a sudden rush of sympathy for the frail little boy. Could he possibly know how many hundreds of seed packets he must sell to buy a burro? Yet Pepe's simple pride and courage brooked no defeat. She promised to return the following day.

As they parted, courage spoke again in Pepe's words, "I am right to help the *papacito* — yes? You see, I am the oldest and almost a man!"

That night, in the dining room of her small hotel, Ruth Sawyer enlisted the help of a compassionate young Jewish scholar who was also staying at the hotel. "We must find some way to help the boy, Abraham," she confided. "He needs so much! Yet he is so proud. It would never do to give him money, even if we could raise enough. It would hurt him terribly. Pepe feels himself to be 'almost a man' — and then there is his pride for the *papacito*."

Next day Abraham went to the park and after meeting and visiting with Pepe they became fast friends. Later, when Abraham rejoined Miss Sawyer, his eyes were glowing.

"Pepe has a secret!" Abraham grinned. "It is a secret shared with thousands of children in Spain. In three days the Three Kings will ride. Ever since Pepe heard that they will ride through Seville, he has believed that they will bring him a burro for his *papacito*. Over and over he told me, 'A present it will be, a *regalo* — a big one — because the *papacito* is such a good man.'"

"At that moment," Ruth Sawyer writes, "I could have shouted for joy! We had never thought of the Kings! So much could be done in their name!"

That evening Abraham climbed upon a chair and addressed the tourists in the hotel dining room. His voice was strong and urgent. "Many of you are strangers here," he began, "but I have a story to tell you about a very small, ill-fed but brave little boy who sleeps on the cold ground under a tree."

Eloquently, Abraham told them of Pepe's love for the *papacito* and of his faith in the goodness of the Three Kings. "Perhaps you think as we did," he concluded, "that because Pepe is a stranger in the city the Three Kings may not know he is here, and so they might not leave the burro. After dinner I will pass my hat around. Anything that you care to give to help the Three Kings remember this small boy, we would greatly appreciate."

Around went the hat. Spanish pesos, English pounds and American dollars went into it. With Miss Sawyer's portion added there was enough to buy everything that was needed.

On Three Kings' Day, the streets and the plaza in Seville were filled with people. Ruth Sawyer stood on tip-toe and little Pepe sat high up on Abraham's shoulders as the Three Kings, riding on splendid stallions, came into view. Caspar and Melchior and Balthazar, wearing golden crowns and gorgeous, brilliantly coloured and jewelled robes, scattered sweets as they rode. There were chocolates and caramels and Turkish delight, all done up in silver and gold paper.

Pepe was quick with his catching and his happy, piping voice often rang out, "I have caught one! Oh, I have caught many!" And above Pepe's voice came the shouting of the crowd, *"Magnífico! Más splendido que nada!"*

When the great procession had ended, Ruth Sawyer and Abraham invited Pepe to a restaurant to celebrate the Feast Day — an invitation that the hungry little boy could not refuse.

As they said good-bye at the park, Abraham gave Pepe a last piece of advice. "Look here, *hombre,* if you still believe that the Kings will bring a burro for the *papacito,* remember this. They are wise men as well as kings and they do not leave even small gifts where boys stay awake watching for them to come."

"I will remember, *amigo.* I will sleep soundly because I believe and because I will be very tired." And with a good-bye wave, Pepe disappeared among the trees.

Late that night, Ruth Sawyer and Abraham slipped into the Parque Maria Luisa and tethered a young, strong burro to a tree opposite the fir tree where Pepe slept. Quietly they laid out a new warm jacket, pants and sturdy shoes; and a wallet with enough money inside to buy food for the boy and the burro on their way home.

Then they stood silently, imagining the joy that would shine on Pepe's face when he awoke in the morning to find what the Three Kings had brought — for the *papacito.* At last, into the darkness, Ruth Sawyer and Abraham whispered the farewell that all good friends in Spain say to those about to set forth on a journey, *"Vaya con Dios, amigo!* Go with God, little friend."

Adapted from a true story by Ruth Sawyer

Candlemas

February 2

Down with the rosemary and bayes
Down with the mistletoe:
Instead of holly, now up-raise
The greener box* (for show)

The holly hitherto did sway,
Let box now domineer
Until the dancing Easter-Day
Or Easter's Eve appear.

Thus times do shift; each thing his turn does hold;
New things succeed, as former things grow old.

In olden times, the last farewells were said to the Christmas Season on Candlemas, February 2. When Jesus was born, it was the custom for every Jewish mother to go to the Temple forty days after her first male child was born and 'present him to the Lord'. At the same time, the mother was 'purified' or 'blessed'. Mary made this trip to the Temple with the Baby Jesus and that is why February 2, the fortieth day after Christmas, is also known as the Festival of the Presentation of Christ in the Temple.

Because this was the first public 'presentation' of Jesus, the Light of the World, many candles are lighted for the celebration of this day. It was also customary to bless the year's supply of candles for the church on this day — hence the name, Candlemas.

Some families like to mark Candlemas Eve by lighting a special candle in the home to 'light the way into the new season'. Sometimes the children are allowed to stay up late — or until the candle burns out.

*The 'greener box' was an old term for the early spring greenery and flowers such as pussywillow and snowdrops. These verses are from 'Ceremonies For Candlemas Eve' by Robert Herrick.
'The Snowdrop' is by Anna Bunston de Bary.

THE SNOWDROP

*Close to the sod
There can be seen
A thought of God
In white and green.*

When the days are darkest the earth enshrines
The seeds of summer's birth.
The spirit of man is a light that shines
Deep in the darkness of earth.

P.S. Moffat

The Loveliest of Lights

I love to look at stars
But on a cloudy night,
We only have the faith that they
Are shining out of sight.

I love to look at candles,
So softly luminous,
But sometimes all the light we have
Is what we have in us.

Our loveliest of lights
Is one we cannot see,
God's steadfast loving abiding
Everlastingly.

James Dillet Freeman

58

Valentine's Day

February 14

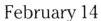

Long before Christianity began, February 14, the day we celebrate as Valentine's Day, fell in the midst of a joyous and somewhat riotous Roman Festival called the 'Lupercalia'. One of the Roman gods honoured during this Festival was Pan or Faunus, the god of nature. Another was Juno, the goddess of women and marriage. During the Lupercalia it was a popular custom for young men to draw the name of a young unmarried woman from a name-box. The two would then be partners or 'sweethearts' during the time of the celebrations.

When the people of Rome became Christians, the name of this holiday was changed to St. Valentine's Day. It honoured two different saints of the same name. Over the years, the legends of these two Valentines have been blended together, creating a story of romance and true love.

The Legend of St. Valentine

The Roman Emperor Claudius II needed soldiers. He felt that marriage made men want to stay at home instead of fighting wars, so he passed a law against marriage.

A kind-hearted young priest, by the name of Valentine, saw the pain that this law caused to the young men and women who loved each other. Secretly he married as many couples as he could before his actions were discovered and he was condemned to death by the Emperor.

While he was in prison awaiting execution, Valentine showed true love and compassion to everyone around him, including his jailer. The jailer had a young daughter who was blind but, through a miracle, Valentine restored her sight. Just before his death in Rome on February 14 he wrote her a farewell message signed, "From your Valentine."

*Doves and Cupids,
Red Hearts and Roses Fair,
Make so Sweet a Valentine,
For Love is in the Air.*

Valentine's Day Customs

Since the first Valentine's Day in 468 A.D., on each February 14, the image of St. Valentine, with his true love for humanity and his willingness to sacrifice, was brought before the people. Love for the old light-hearted customs and celebrations of the Lupercalia was strong, however, and many of them persisted right through the Middle Ages. Even to this day our Valentine decorations bear an ancient symbol of love — Roman cupids with their bows and love-arrows.

Yet perhaps St. Valentine has done his work after all, for this day, although no longer celebrated by churches, has taken on a much broader idea of *true love*. It is a day when not only sweethearts, but families and friends express love and affection to each other. Today, nearly everyone loves Valentine's Day and feels better for giving or receiving those wonderful Valentine greetings — for whatever their words or verses may say, they all carry the message:

Roses are Red,
Violets are Blue,
You're very Special!
I Care about You!

The Easter Story

Retold from the Gospels of Matthew, Mark, Luke and John

Three years had passed since Jesus was baptised in the River Jordan and the prophet John saw the Dove descend upon Him. Twelve men had been chosen by Jesus to be His special disciples and to travel with Him. Jesus taught and preached; He healed the sick, He performed miracles! Everywhere He went, crowds gathered to hear Him speak. Many hailed Him as the Messiah, the Saviour for whom the Jews had waited so long.

There were others, however, who were His enemies. Many of the priests and rulers of the Jews did not believe that He was the Messiah. They were afraid of His influence upon the people. They accused Jesus of breaking the laws of their religion.

On the Sunday before the Jewish Feast of the Passover, that day which we now call Palm Sunday, Jesus was on His way to Jerusalem. Crowds of people lined the roads waving palm branches and crying, "Hosanna! Blessed is He who comes in the name of the Lord." Joyfully they laid a carpet of clothing and palm branches on the road for Jesus to ride upon and many, many people followed Him into the city.

All Jerusalem was filled with wonder as Jesus taught each day in the courtyard of the Holy Temple. When his enemies saw the crowds around Him, they became even more frightened. They wanted to stop Jesus from teaching but they did not dare for he was surrounded by so many friendly people.

On the Thursday after Palm Sunday, Jesus and His disciples came together to share the Feast of the Passover. Jesus knew that it would be His last supper. He knew, too, that one of His own disciples, Judas Iscariot, would betray Him.

During the supper, Jesus took bread and wine. He gave thanks for them and shared them with His disciples. He told them that they should continue to do this *in remembrance of Him* — that the bread was His body, given for mankind — that the wine was His blood, shed for many that their sins might be taken away.

Jesus then rose from the table. He took a basin of water and lovingly washed the feet of each of the disciples. "This is how you, too, should serve one another," He told them.

After the supper, Jesus with His disciples went to a garden called Gethsemane, which was a short distance from the city.

"My soul is filled with sorrow for what is to come," He told the disciples. "Stay, watch with me while I pray." But the disciples soon fell asleep. Jesus, alone in the world, prayed to His Father in Heaven. And an Angel came and gave Him strength.

Great Ra-pha-el, Archangel bright,
Sends down pure rays of healing light;
As springtime comes and greens the earth
And out of darkness comes new birth,
God's healing Angel lights our way
To understand His Word this day.

Suddenly the stillness of the night was shattered by the sound of voices. A group of Temple guards, led by Judas Iscariot, burst into the garden. The disciples awoke and tried to defend their Master, but Jesus told them not to. He allowed the guards to arrest Him.

Jesus was taken before a council of priests. They said He was guilty of speaking against things which they held most sacred. They condemned Him and brought Him before the Roman Governor, Pontius Pilate.

Although Pontius Pilate wanted to spare His life, the enemies of Jesus cried out, "Crucify Him. Crucify Him." Pontius Pilate then gave the order for Jesus Christ to be crucified.

All this happened on Friday, the day which we now call Good Friday, meaning 'God's Friday'. On that day, Jesus was whipped, insulted and mocked by the Roman soldiers. Then, weak and suffering, He was made to carry the heavy cross to a hill outside the city, called Calvary or Golgotha. There, between two thieves, Jesus Christ was crucified. Yet in spite of all His suffering, He prayed aloud, "Father, forgive them, for they know not what they do."

After Jesus knew that He had accomplished everything that was necessary to fulfil the prophecies in the scriptures, He said, "It is finished." And His Spirit left His body.

At that moment the earth trembled. There was a great earthquake. In places the earth opened and rocks split in two.

Before sunset, Jesus' lifeless body was taken from the cross by His friends. They wrapped His body in fine linen cloth and placed it in a tomb. A large stone was placed in front of the entrance and the tomb was sealed.

Very early on Sunday morning, even before dawn, the sorrowful friends of Jesus, singly and in small groups, groped their way through the darkness toward His tomb.

Near sunrise, as some of the women who loved Jesus came to the tomb, there was another earthquake. The Angel of the Lord appeared and rolled away the stone from the entrance of the tomb. The Angel's face shone like lightning and he was clothed in brilliant white.

The Angel said to the women, "Don't be afraid. I know that you are seeking Jesus — but He is not here for He is risen!"

And when the women looked into the tomb, it was empty!

"Go quickly," said that Angel of the Lord, "tell the disciples that Jesus is risen from the dead!"

That same evening, when the disciples were gathered together, Jesus suddenly appeared in their midst. The wonder, the love, the joy of knowing that He was risen stayed with the disciples all their lives. And through them, the Easter message spread throughout the world — and is still the same today: Jesus is Risen! Jesus Christ Lives!

Easter

Sunrise! Light! Triumph! Rejoice! Life! These are words which spring quickly to our minds on Easter Morning. Easter 'Season' is the time for the *re-member-ing* — the putting together again — of the supreme deed of Jesus Christ. Through this deed, going through the experience of death and then raising up the human body once more, Jesus Christ has given mankind the promise of Eternal Life.

Easter Time is often thought of as the days leading up to Easter Sunday. However, the Christian Calendar established the forty days before Easter Sunday as the period called Lent* which is traditionally a time of spiritual preparation for Easter.

Easter Time, or Easter Season, is really the forty days after Easter Sunday. It begins with that joy-filled day when Jesus Christ rose from the dead and continues through to Ascension, forty days later. That is when the Risen Christ made his last earthly appearance to the Disciples and 'ascended' into 'the clouds.'

Ten days after Ascension, at Whitsun, the Holy Spirit came to the Apostles and inspired them to go forth into the world and perform their great works. Whitsun is also known as Pentecost. Taken together, Lent, Easter Sunday, and Ascension, followed by Whitsun, cover more than ninety days! Celebrating each of these periods of a larger Easter Season brings a special blessing to each of us.

The forty days of Lent do not include Sundays, which are always considered Feast days, not Fast days; because on Sunday, Jesus Christ rose from the dead.

Celebrations Before Lent Begins

Shrove Tuesday

From the earliest years of Christianity, Lent has been the time of self-examination, self-denial and self-discipline. The day before Lent was originally named Shrove Tuesday because it was on that day that the 'Shriving Bell' rang, summoning everyone to church to be 'shriven' — to confess his sins before beginning the serious preparation for Easter. In olden days, celebrating Lent also meant fasting; that is, not eating any food on certain days and not eating certain foods on any days. Eggs, meat, milk and rich buttery dishes were the principal foods to be avoided. Because of that, Shrove Tuesday became known by other names as well!

Fat Tuesday

"Waste not, want not!" is an old and famous family rule! It had a special meaning because in the days before anyone even dreamed of a refrigerator or ice-box, certain foods spoiled quickly. Being merry while 'eating it all up' became the custom of Shrove Tuesday. Since many of the foods eaten were fatty, buttery and rich (besides making one fat, of course) this merry feasting day became known as Fat Tuesday! But wait, Shrove Tuesday has still more names . . .

Pancake Day

One way to use up eggs, milk and fats is to combine them with flour and to make pancakes. And for hundreds of years, that's just what villagers and town folk alike have done. In England, Shrove Tuesday became so well known as Pancake Day that even the Shriving Bell was transformed into the Pancake Bell, signalling the beginning of feasting and holiday fun. Today in some English and American towns*, at the stroke of the Pancake Bell, women still gather in the town square to begin a Pancake Race. Each woman carries a hot frying-pan containing a freshly cooked pancake which she must toss into the air three times, while racing to the village church. A poem by Eleanor Farjeon illustrates this custom:

> Run to the Church with a frying-pan,
> Never you lose a minute!
> Run to the Church with a frying-pan
> And a yellow pancake in it.
> > First to carry her pancake there,
> > Though heavy or light she beat it,
> > Must toss her cake to the Bellringer,
> > And the Bellringer must eat it.
> > > Then be she madam or be she miss
> > > All breathless after rushing,
> > > The Bellringer shall give her his kiss
> > > And never mind her blushing.

Carnival, Carnival!

The very word 'Carnival' brings to each of us a riot of images — crowds of merry-makers in the streets, pirates and clowns, a King and Queen of Carnival riding on flower-covered floats in colourful parades; glittering costume balls — laughing, shouting, dancing, singing — feasting! In many Spanish-, Portugese-, Italian- and French-speaking countries, Carnival celebrations sometimes last for many days, beginning as early as February and growing more and more boisterious until they reach their peak on Shrove Tuesday. The word carnival comes from the Latin words *carnem levare* which means 'to put away flesh'. This festive time is also called *Mardi Gras* which is French for Fat Tuesday. The most famous of these celebrations take place each year in America's New Orleans, Louisiana, and in Brazil's Rio de Janeiro.

> It's Carnival! It's Mardi Gras!
> The merry maskers shout, "Hurrah!"
> And crowd through streets in costumes bright;
> They laugh and sing both day and night.
> At balls so gay they feast and dance
> As if this were life's final chance —
> > For soon begins another phase —
> > A different mood, the Lenten Days —
> > A time to turn from worldly din;
> > To quiet down and look within.
> > But till Ash Wednesday ends the ball —
> > It's Mardi Gras — It's Carnival!

*Since 1950, Olney, in Buckinghamshire, England, and Liberal, in Kansas, U.S.A., race each other every year, competing for the fastest time.

Ash Wednesday and Lent

Easter is the oldest and most important Christian Festival for it celebrates the supreme message of Christianity — the Resurrection of Jesus Christ. Each year another life-renewing experience can come to us at Easter, especially when we prepare our minds and hearts to receive it.

By the year 400 A.D. the early Christian church had established a forty-day period of preparation which we call Lent. The word Lent comes from the Old English word for spring. Literally Lent means that time of the year when the days *lengthen.* Spring has not yet come, but it is on its way.

Lent has always been a time of self-examination, and of self-discipline. During the Middle Ages, however, the rules for celebration of Lent were so strict that many people dreaded the season. Gradually the Lenten demands and restrictions were relaxed. In more modern times, most Christians see Lent not as a time of self-punishment but as a time for strengthening oneself through developing deeper understanding, love and faith.

Although strict Lenten fasts are seldom observed today, many people still give up a favourite food or activity during this time. Others strive to give up old habits such as thinking of 'me first', or fault finding. Still others try to train themselves to be more thankful for what they have. Some seek out opportunities to praise other people as well as to set aside regular times for giving thanks to the Lord and studying the life of Jesus.

Ash Wednesday

The first day of Lent is named Ash Wednesday. In nature many things have to wither and decay and *turn to ash* before new life can spring forth. Early Christians held that before each person can experience the new life of Easter Time, he has to let some of his faults and bad habits die away and thus 'turn to ash'.

Ancient peoples scattered ashes over their heads in sorrow and some wore 'sackcloth and ashes' to publicly announce that they had sinned and wanted forgiveness. Many Christian churches still use ash at the beginning of Lent to remind people to repent; that is, to be sorry for their mistakes, to change their way of thinking and look for ways to be better and stronger.

Some churches hold special services on Ash Wednesday, during which a cross is marked in ash on the forehead of each member of the congregation. The ashes are made from palm leaves which have been saved from the previous year's Palm Sunday service. The ash is a reminder that when we die, our bodies then decay and turn to ash. The cross can be a reminder, however, that the spirit exists forever. Although Jesus died on the cross, His Spirit was able to raise up His body from death.

Out of the Ashes

There is an ancient legend about the Phoenix, a great and wonderful bird with glossy, coloured plumage which lived in Arabia. Only a single Phoenix was on earth at any one time and it lived for five to six hundred years. When the time came for this magical bird to die, it built a nest from frankincense, myrrh, spices and herbs. The Phoenix would then set fire to its nest and die within the flames. But out of the ashes would arise a new Phoenix who would carry the bones of the old Phoenix to an altar built by man and dedicated to the sun.

Early Christians used this story of the Phoenix as a symbol of the resurrection of Jesus who died, then rose again to life.

Lenten Customs

From many countries come different folk customs which have been celebrated during the Lenten season throughout the ages. From France comes the tradition of making a Lenten Calendar which looks like a little nun. Even today drawing and cutting out this quaint figure is a project which can be enjoyed by the entire family on Ash Wednesday. It will also serve as a Lenten reminder throughout the season.

Long before regular calendars were in common use, French children made a paper nun with seven feet to mark off the seven weeks of Lent. As each week passed, a foot was folded back under the nun's gown. This drawing of the nun does not have a mouth. That is because French children never gave her one. It reminded them that Lent was a time of fasting.

Another custom, a delicious one, that is associated with Ash Wednesday is eating pretzels!

During the early Christian years when fasting was an important part of Lent, eggs, milk and fats were not allowed. Since pretzels contain only flour, water and salt they were eaten instead of bread, during Lent. Bakers even twisted the pretzel dough to represent two arms crossed in the act of prayer. In fact, the German name *pretzel* is from a Latin word meaning 'little arms'.

It's fun to bake pretzels at home, but home-made or store-bought, serving pretzels is a custom which the whole family can share to celebrate the first day of Lent.

Realities

Spring's Not Yet Here

As Lent begins with trees still bare,
There's hardly a new leaf anywhere;
But on the branch, if you look well,
Beneath the bark there's a gentle swell,
Where rising life begins to flood
And promises that new leaves will bud.
Then, warmed by sun and fed by rain,
All that seemed dead will bloom again.

Reality

My thoughts are very potent things,
They hem me in or give me wings.
My thoughts create, enslave, or free,
Enrich, or they impoverish me.
My own thoughts make me glad or sad,
They choose, decide, for good or bad,
Whate'er they be, is true for me.
My thoughts are my reality.

Viola Lukaweicki

A Word

When a word that we have wrought
Flowers in another's thought,
When it ripens to a seed
As another's living deed —
Then an angel picks it up,
Places it in heaven's cup,
Smiles, that such sweet grain has grown,
Keeps it till it may be sown —
And from such kernels makes the bread
With which — all mankind is fed.

Arvia Mackaye Ege

Who Has Seen the Wind?

Who has seen the wind?
Neither you nor I;
But when the trees bow down their heads
The wind is passing by.

Christina G. Rossetti

Lady of the Brightly Coloured Eggs

Each country has its own Easter Egg traditions and its own favourite stories about how those traditions began. One story tells that during the Crusades, Lady Rosalind, the daughter of the Duke of Burgundy, was forced to flee from her castle which was under attack by a neighbouring Lord. Her husband, Lord Arno, was away fighting in Palestine.

Lady Rosalind and her young children, accompanied by a loyal servant, found their way to a small village in a valley hidden away in the mountains. The people there were very kind and even provided them with a house. The lady wanted in some way to repay the villagers.

Chickens had originally been brought to Europe from Asia but had not yet reached this isolated valley. Lady Rosalind sent her servant on the long trip over the mountains to purchase some, and soon both chickens and eggs were plentiful in the village.

When Easter came, Lady Rosalind boiled eggs and coloured their shells blue and red and yellow, using dyes made from roots, berries and moss. She hid the eggs in little straw nests outside her cottage and invited the village children to an egg hunt. Soon Lady Rosalind was known as the Lady of the Brightly Coloured Eggs.

When Lord Arno returned from the Crusades, the noble family was happily reunited. And every Easter thereafter, Lady Rosalind sent many brightly coloured eggs to the children of the village which had been so kind to her. In time, the custom of giving coloured eggs spread throughout the land and to every other Christian country.

The Easter Fires of Fredericksburg

It was Easter Eve, 1847, in the newly formed American settlement of Fredericksburg in Texas. Indian camp-fires blazed on the hills all around the little colony of settlers who had recently come from Germany.

In a small cabin within the settlement two young children cried out in alarm as they noticed the fires. Hoping to calm them, their mother quickly recalled two stories from her homeland; the story of the Easter Rabbit and a tale of fairies who dance around fires on certain spring and summer nights.

"The Easter Rabbit and his fairy helpers are surely at work in the hills this night," she told the children. "They are cooking eggs in giant cauldrons over those huge bonfires and colouring them with pretty dyes made from wild flowers." The children were delighted with this explanation and soon settled down to dream of the Easter Rabbit.

Meanwhile, the leaders of the settlement were concluding a successful treaty with the Indians. Soon they returned to Fredericksburg. When they heard the story that the young mother had told to her children, they pledged that each year thereafter, on the night before Easter, they would light fires on the hills as a thankful memorial to their successful treaty with the Indians. And to this day, on Easter Eve, boys and girls, descendants of the original settlers, kindle the Easter Fires of Fredericksburg.

Forty Hours, Forty Days, Forty Years

There are forty days of Lent (not counting Sundays), from Ash Wednesday until Easter Morning. In many languages the name for this Lenten period is from the Latin word for forty, *Quadraginta.* In Italian it is *Quaresima,* in Spanish, *Cuaresma,* in French, *Carême* and in Irish it is *Corghas.*

The forty days of Lent recall the forty hours that Jesus was in the tomb between Good Friday and Easter Morning. We are reminded, too, of the forty days that Jesus fasted during His temptation in the wilderness.

There are many other references to the number forty in the Bible, including the forty days that Moses fasted before he received the Ten Commandments and the forty years that the people of Israel wandered in the desert before entering the Promised Land. Noah's Ark was tossed upon the waters of the flood for forty days. And the Risen Christ walked with His disciples for forty days between Easter and Ascension.

In ancient times, each number was felt to be an expression of God and to reveal a certain aspect of God and His world. The early Church Fathers held that the number forty, when applied to time — forty hours, forty days, forty years — is the necessary period for cleansing or testing and strengthening which allows the *fullness of wisdom* to become *reality.*

The Moon, the Sun, and the Earth — Fixing the Date for Easter

The moon, as well as the sun, has a powerful effect upon the earth and upon the life of man. Some ancient people, such as the Hebrews, felt this so strongly that they based their calendars upon the rhythms of the moon. We call these calendars 'lunar' calendars. Other people, including the Romans, based their calendars on the sun*.

Christianity began in the Holy Land, where people used the lunar calendar. When Christianity was taken to Rome, establishing certain dates became difficult. The results were often confusing because the Romans used the sun calendar. Early church leaders, both Jewish and Roman, agreed that everything to do with the coming of Jesus Christ had been prepared, even the position of the sun, the moon and the stars. They could not agree, however, on how to fix the date for the yearly celebration of Easter. Then, in the fourth century, with the help of astronomers who took into account the position of both the moon and the sun in relation to the earth, a decision was made. At last it was accepted that Easter would always be celebrated on the first Sunday after the full moon that follows the Spring Equinox (March 20 or 21). That is why Easter falls anytime between March 22 and April 25.

The Gregorian calendar, which we use today and which is in widest use throughout the world, is based on the Roman (sun) calendar.

The Selfish Giant

Every afternoon, as they were coming from school, the children would go to the Giant's garden.

It was a large, lovely garden, with soft green grass. Here and there in the grass stood beautiful flowers like stars; and there were twelve peach trees that in the springtime broke out into delicate blossoms, and in the autumn bore rich fruit.

The birds sang so sweetly that the children used to stop their games to listen to them. "How happy we are here!" they cried to one another.

One day the Giant returned from a visit to his friend, the Cornish Ogre, where he had stayed for seven years. When he arrived home, he saw the children playing in the garden.

"What are you doing here?" he cried in a very gruff voice. The children ran away. "My own garden is my own garden," said the Giant, "and I will allow nobody to play in it but myself." So he built a high wall all around it, and put up a notice board: TRESPASSERS WILL BE PROSECUTED.

He was a very selfish giant.

The poor children had nowhere to play. They tried to play in the road, but the road was dusty and full of hard stones, and they did not like it. "How happy we were in the garden!" they said to one another.

Then Spring came, and all over the country there were little blossoms and little birds. But in the garden of the Selfish Giant it was still Winter. The birds did not care to sing in it as there were no children, and the trees forgot to blossom.

Once a beautiful flower put its head out from the snow, but when it saw the notice board it was so sorry for the children that it slipped back into the ground again, and went off to sleep. Only Snow and Frost were pleased. "Spring has forgotten this garden," they cried.

Snow covered up the grass with her great white cloak, and Frost painted all the trees silver. Then North Wind came to stay with them and roared all day about the garden. "This is a delightful spot," he said. "We must invite Hail."

So Hail came with his icy breath, and rattled the roof of the castle.

"I wonder why Spring is so late in coming," said the Selfish Giant.

But Spring never came, nor Summer. Autumn gave golden fruit to every garden, but to the Giant's garden she gave none. "He is too selfish," she said. So it was always Winter there.

One morning the Giant was lying awake in bed when he heard some lovely music. It was only a little linnet singing outside his window, but it was so long since he had heard a bird sing in his garden that it seemed to him to be the most beautiful music in the world.

Then Hail stopped dancing on the roof, and North Wind ceased roaring. The Giant jumped out of bed and looked out.

He saw the most beautiful sight. Through a small hole in the wall the children had crept into the garden, and they were sitting in the branches of the trees. And the trees were so glad to have the children back again that they had covered themselves with blossoms. The birds were twittering and the flowers were looking up through the green grass and laughing.

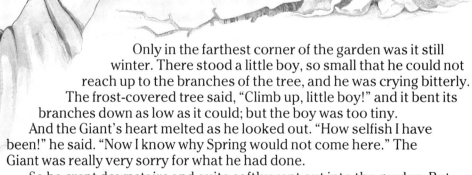

Only in the farthest corner of the garden was it still winter. There stood a little boy, so small that he could not reach up to the branches of the tree, and he was crying bitterly. The frost-covered tree said, "Climb up, little boy!" and it bent its branches down as low as it could; but the boy was too tiny.

And the Giant's heart melted as he looked out. "How selfish I have been!" he said. "Now I know why Spring would not come here." The Giant was really very sorry for what he had done.

So he crept downstairs and quite softly went out into the garden. But when the children saw him, they were so frightened that they all ran away, and Winter came to the garden again. Only the little boy did not run, for his eyes were so full of tears that he did not see the Giant. The Giant strode up behind him and took him gently in his hand, and put him up into the tree.

The tree broke at once into blossom, and the birds came and sang in it

and the little boy stretched out his two arms and flung them around the Giant's neck, and kissed him. And the other children, when they saw the Giant was not wicked, came running back; and with them came Spring.

"It is your garden now, little children — forever," said the Giant, and he took a great axe and knocked down the wall. And when the people were going to market at twelve o'clock, they found the Giant playing with the children in the most beautiful garden they had ever seen.

All day long the children played, and in the evening they came to the Giant to bid him goodbye.

"But where is your little companion?" he said. "The boy I put in the tree." The Giant loved him best because the boy had kissed him.

"We don't know. We have never seen him before," answered the children. "He has gone away." The Giant felt very sad.

Every afternoon when school was over, the children came and played with the Giant. But the little boy whom the Giant loved was never seen again. "How I long to see him," he would say.

Years went by, and the Giant grew old and feeble. He could not play, so he sat and watched the children at their games. "I have many beautiful flowers," he said, "but the children are the most beautiful flowers of all."

One winter morning he looked out of his window. He did not hate Winter now, for he knew that it was merely Spring asleep, and that the flowers were resting.

Suddenly he rubbed his eyes in wonder, for in the farthest corner of the garden was a tree quite covered with lovely white blossoms. And underneath stood the little boy he had loved.

Out into the garden ran the Giant, in great joy. But when he came quite close to the child his face grew red with anger, and he said, "Who dareth to wound thee?" For on the palms of the child's hands were the prints of two nails, and the prints of two nails on the child's little feet.

"Who hath dared to wound thee?" cried the Giant. "Tell me, that I may take my big sword and slay him."

"Nay!" answered the child. "For these are the wounds of Love."

"Who are you?" asked the Giant, and a strange awe fell on him, and he knelt before the little child.

And the child smiled on the Giant and said, "Once you let me play in your garden; today you shall come with me to my garden, which is Paradise."

And when the children ran in that afternoon, they found the Giant lying dead under the tree, all covered with white blossoms.

Adapted and abridged from the story by Oscar Wilde

71

St. Patrick and the Easter Fires

March 17 — St. Patrick's Day

The moon and the stars were hidden behind a thick blanket of clouds as Bishop Patrick, carrying an unlighted torch, stepped out of a crudely built stone church. Waiting in the darkness were Irish tribesmen who had now accepted Christianity. Here were men and women, who until only a short time before had been fierce, warlike followers of the Druid priests.

Legend tells that even after the clansmen accepted Christianity, they did not want to give up their spring custom of lighting fires to welcome the return of the sun. Bishop Patrick, however, wisely offered them a new Christian fire ceremony. Together, on Easter Eve, they lit huge bonfires outside the church and together they watched and prayed in memory of Jesus Christ's journey through the darkness of the underworld, which led to His final victory as He rose from the dead on Easter Morning.

In the years that followed, the custom of lighting and blessing a new fire on Easter Eve spread throughout Europe. Then the bonfires gave way to 'Paschal candles', which even today are lit in churches all over the world to herald the miracle of Easter.

Bishop Patrick became St. Patrick, the great saint of Ireland; and March 17, the day he died, is celebrated wherever Irish people live.

The story of this great man is known partly through history and partly through legend. Patrick was born in Britain to Christian parents near the beginning of the fifth century. When only sixteen, he was captured by Irish raiders and taken to Ireland. There he lived among the warlike clans who practised pagan rites until, with God's help, he was able to escape.

Once home in Britain, Patrick had a vision about returning to Ireland. He studied hard, became a Bishop of the church and was sent back to Ireland. There, Patrick's life was in constant danger from the clan chieftains and their Druid priests, who feared the coming of Christianity. Still, Bishop Patrick bravely preached the Gospels and eventually led Ireland to embrace the Christian religion.

It is said that Patrick often used the shamrock as a symbol of the Trinity — the Father, Son and Holy Spirit — explaining as he held up a shamrock how there could be 'Three in One and One in Three'.

Legends also credit St. Patrick with driving all snakes from Ireland and performing many other miracles. One of his greatest achievements, however, is an historical fact. In addition to building churches he founded monasteries, and St. Patrick taught the Irish clergy to read Latin. As time went on the monasteries, with their libraries, became important centres for learning and culture. Years later, when Europe was overrun by barbarians, it was largely due to the work begun by St. Patrick that learning was kept alive while the rest of the Western World lay in ignorance.

Mothering Sunday — Mother's Day

Mother Church, Mother Earth, Mother of the Gods — our human mothers — all of them have been part of the celebration of 'Mothering Sunday' — as the fourth Sunday in Lent is affectionately known.

Long before Christian times, great festivals were held every spring to honour Rhea or Cybele, Mother of all the Gods. Festivals dedicated to Mother Earth were also joyfully celebrated. With the coming of Christianity, a new springtime celebration honouring the 'Mother Church' took their place.

During the Middle Ages there were no schools where trades could be learned. Young people often had to travel far from home to live and work at the shop of master craftsmen who taught them their skills. These young people, as well as 'live-in' servants, were allowed only one holiday a year on which to visit their families — which is how 'Mothering Sunday' got its name. For this special day of family rejoicing, the Lenten fast was broken. In some places the Day was even called 'Refreshment Day' or 'Simnel Day' because of the sweet cakes called 'Simnel Cakes' which were traditionally eaten on that day.

Mother's Day is often confused with Mothering Sunday; however, they are quite different. Early in this century churches in the United States began to hold special Mother's Day services. These were prompted by the tireless efforts of an American woman from West Virginia, Anna Jarvis.

In 1914, due to her perseverance, President Woodrow Wilson declared a national Mother's Day to be celebrated each year in the United States, on the second Sunday of May — "as a public expression of our love and reverence for the mothers of our country." Since that time, the American way of celebrating Mother's Day has spread to countries all over the world.

The Easter Tree

It was the night of her eighth birthday and Julie was leaving her mum and dad and the house in the small village where she had been born.

Julie was determined not to cry when Aunt Linda arrived to take her to stay in the big city apartment where she lived. Julie's mother had been so ill that the doctors insisted she must go away for several months, to a special hospital where she could be taken care of and have complete rest.

"We'll all be together again soon, darling," Father said as he kissed Julie goodbye. She wanted to hold her father tight and to tell him how scared she was, for herself and for Mum; but he said, "I know what a big, brave girl you are, Julie. I'm so proud of you."

Julie choked back her tears and Father closed the car door. Aunt Linda started the engine and down the road they went into the night.

Nine weeks later Julie had still not shed one tear. But neither could she smile and it took all the courage she could muster to hide her growing fear. Aunt Linda tried to make her feel at home but Julie couldn't respond. The constant business and noise of the large city frightened her — and at her new school, Julie was miserable. The big city children did not go out of their way to make friends with the shy little girl and, though Julie had formerly been a good student, she now found it impossible to concentrate. She feared she was going to fail!

Aunt Linda felt Julie's unhappiness and knew that it was more than just being homesick! But when she tried to get Julie to talk about her feelings, a polite, "I'm really fine, thank you," was the little girl's only answer. Yet, as the days passed, school grew even more terrifying for Julie and she began to have frequent nightmares — until, mercifully, spring holiday began.

The very next morning, Aunt Linda entered Julie's room. She was smiling and she looked different, somehow. She put her arms around the child and asked gently, "Julie . . . do you pray?"

"Sometimes," the little girl said softly as she turned away from her aunt's gaze.

"Me too," Aunt Linda said, "just sometimes. But you know what? I've started praying and I'm going to keep on praying! God made this world too beautiful for us to just mope around in it! Soon it will be Easter and I am praying that, somehow, this will be a wonderful Easter — for you, for me and for your mum and dad.

"You needn't tell me right now, Julie," Aunt Linda continued, "but I'd be awfully glad if you'd pray with me. You know, Jesus did say, 'Where two or more are gathered in my name, there I am in their midst'. Seems to me that's a pretty powerful promise."

Suddenly Aunt Linda gave Julie an extra strong hug and said, with a grin, "Now, young lady, let's get our jackets. We're going into the country to find an Easter tree!"

Julie was curious but it took nearly an hour of riding through the beautiful green countryside before she asked timidly, "What's an Easter tree?"

Aunt Linda laughed out loud — a really joyful laugh. "I thought you'd never ask, dear! An Easter tree is something I learned about when I was your age. I always wanted to make one, but I never did. Now I will because I have you to help me."

As they drove, Aunt Linda described an Easter tree as a well-shaped branch, 'planted' in a brightly coloured painted pot and hung with Easter 'symbols' — a little toy rabbit, a lamb, baby ducks, real Easter eggs, brightly coloured sweets and magazine pictures or hand drawings of Easter flowers and bells and butterflies. "And the really fun part," Aunt Linda went on enthusiastically, "is that as we hang the Easter symbols on the tree, one of us can read up on what each one means and tell the other!"

Just then Aunt Linda pulled the car off to the side of the road and stopped. Soon she and Julie were picking their way through a thick grove of trees. "I'm sure we'll find just the right branch to be our Easter tree," Aunt Linda announced cheerfully. Of course, she made sure that Julie was the one who found the 'perfect' branch.

Later, after several stops, breathless and tired, they manoeuvred their 'tree' into the living room of the apartment. One of their stops had been to the Public Library where they had come away with an armful of Easter books.

That evening they 'planted' their branch in a big pot filled with damp sand. "Terrific," Aunt Linda said, "it looks bare right now but our Easter tree will soon come to life. Our first symbol is the tree itself! I'll read up on this one. Now it's your turn to choose a symbol to hang on our tree. What will it be — an egg, a lamb, a rabbit?"

For a second, Julie's eyes lit up with joy as she pictured the funny, cuddly little white rabbits she'd often held in her arms while visiting Mr. Jenkins' farm. But before she could answer, her face clouded as a picture flashed into her mind, the picture of her mother lying in a far off hospital room — all alone!

Julie stood very still, unable to speak, lost in the confused world of her own feelings — of loss and fear and guilt all mixed up together.

Aunt Linda seemed to understand for she took hold of the little girl's hand and just waited patiently until at last Julie stammered, "D-do you think Mum would like it if I drew p-pictures of our Easter tree and wrote about the symbols? D-do you think she'd like to know about them, too?"

Aunt Linda smiled through the sudden tears that sprang into her eyes, "Why, Julie, I think that's the most beautiful idea I've ever heard."

Aunt Linda began to cry then, and so did Julie — great sobs that felt so good because they'd been held in for so long.

Later, their tears brushed away, Julie and Aunt Linda looked at their little Easter tree standing there — so bare and forlorn — yet so full of promise. And all at once they began to laugh, almost at the same instant, as if some magic presence had touched them.

"That poor tree needs a rabbit," Julie giggled. "Let's hang an Easter bunny on our Easter tree!"

Julie and Aunt Linda prayed together that night and every day from then on for Mum to get well — and in thankfulness. They made their Easter tree and drew pictures and wrote little stories and sent them to Mum. And she became well and strong again, even faster than the doctors expected. To this day she says it was the message of the Easter tree that did it.

Easter Symbols

The Easter Egg

Hens' eggs, chocolate eggs, eggs of marshmallow and marzipan; dyed eggs, painted eggs — eggs with an endless variety of designs and in every colour of the rainbow — eggs made of china and porcelain, eggs fashioned by famous artists and covered with precious jewels — all of these are part of our modern celebration of Easter.

Even before Jesus walked on earth, the egg was a symbol for new life. Just imagine! From out of a lifeless shell, a tiny beak appears, then a fuzzy head — the small warm body of a living baby bird. What a miracle of new life!

People *felt* this miracle. They wanted to stress its magic. What better symbol could there be for the magic-miracle quality of new life than brightly coloured and decorated eggs? And what better egg-bringer could there be than a magic hare or rabbit who always avoids being seen?

Early Christians shared this magical feeling of hope that comes in spring as new miracles of life occur. But they *knew* of an even greater miracle! Jesus Christ had come through death to rise to life again in the springtime and to walk and talk with His disciples. For Christians, eggs became a symbol, not only of *new* life, but of the power of resurrection by which Jesus Christ *came forth* from the tomb. It is also a symbol for their own rebirth in Him.

The Rabbit and the Hare

Thousands upon thousands — literally millions of furry little rabbits are born each year — all over the world. Perhaps this is why rabbits and hares have always been symbols for abundant life and have long been part of joyful springtime celebrations.

To Our Easter Bunny

O cuddly bunny, silky white,
With pink-tinged eyes so quick and bright,
Or forest hare, that seen by night,
Oft glistens in the pale moonlight;
You both conspire to fill our dreams
With candied eggs and jelly beans —
And sometimes — tho' it's kind of funny,
We hope you'll leave a choc'late bunny!
You used to leave just eggs, we're told,
But that was in the days of old,
Still — tho' our baskets now hold sweets,
We never see you leave these treats!
For when on Easter Morn we wake,
We find you've gone before daybreak!
O Easter bunny, please don't fear,
We'd never harm you, you're too dear.
So won't you come this year and stay —
And spend with us an Easter Day!

The Cross

Throughout the world and among people everywhere, the cross is accepted as the sign of Christianity and carries with it *two* powerful meanings. Because Jesus died upon the cross, the cross has become a symbol of suffering, of trials and of obstacles to be overcome. However, as Jesus went through death on the cross, the Holy Spirit flowed into the earth and into all mankind. Through His Resurrection, Jesus Christ gave to all men and women who will receive it, the promise of resurrection. And so the cross is also the Christian sign of faith and hope. It is the promise of Eternal Life.

The Lamb

Little lamb, who made thee?
Dost thou know who made thee?
Gave thee life, and bade thee feed
By the streams and o'er the mead;
Gave thee clothing of delight,
Softest clothing, woolly, bright;
Gave thee such a tender voice,
Making all the vales rejoice:
Little lamb, who made thee?
Dost thou know who made thee?

Little lamb, I'll tell thee,
Little lamb, I'll tell thee;
He is callèd by thy name,
For He calls Himself a lamb;
He is meek, and he is mild,
He became a little child.
I a child, and thou a lamb,
We are callèd by His name
Little lamb, God bless thee,
Little lamb, God bless thee.

William Blake

Gentle, mild, meek, patient . . . these are words we use to describe the little lamb. In the old Hebrew religion, the lamb was often used as a sacrifice to God because it was believed to be *pure.* When John the Baptist beheld Jesus, he said, "Behold, the Lamb of God." The early Christians, many of whom were Jews, understood that John had meant that the pure life of Jesus would be sacrificed to take away sin. In the Christian church, the lamb became the Easter Lamb, a symbol of Jesus and His sacrifice.

78

The Sun

Everything that lives on earth needs light and warmth. To ancient man, the sun, which gives so freely of its light and warmth, was the natural picture for the heavenly, life-giving Spirit of Light. For Christians, Jesus Christ is the Spirit of Light come to earth and they likened Him to the sun. In the English language even the words 'sun' and 'Son' are related. There is an old saying that when Christ was born, "The sun became the Son."

Ancient people also said that the sun dies each night and is reborn in the morning. The early Christians used a picture of the rising sun as a symbol for Christ's Resurrection.

Flowers

The little flowers came through the ground
At Easter time, at Easter time;
They raised their heads and looked around
At happy Easter time.
And every pretty bud did say,
"Good people, bless this holy day,
for Christ is risen, the angels say,
At happy Easter time!"

Stanza from 'Easter Time' by Laura E. Richards

The Butterfly

One of our best loved symbols for death and resurrection is the butterfly.

Waken, sleeping butterfly,
Burst your narrow prison.
Spread your golden wings and rise —
Christ the Lord is risen;
Spread your wings and tell the story,
How He rose, the Lord of glory!

When the Root Children Wake Up

All winter long the trees are bare, the wind is cold and the fields are empty.

But very early in the Spring the sun begins to grow warmer, the air softer and the sky bluer. And boys and girls grow happier, though they cannot tell just why.

Down underground something is happening.

Something secret and wonderful.

The root children, who have been sleeping soundly all Winter, are awakened by the Earth Mother. She comes with her candle and her little firefly helpers to tell them they must be up and at work, for it will soon be Spring. They are very sleepy at first but soon begin to stretch and open their eyes and be glad that it is time to wake.

Wide awake at last, in their root house, the root girls work busily on their new Spring dresses. Each chooses the colour she loves best — violet, yellow, blue, white, orange or red — and with needle, thread and thimble, sews happily till her work is done.

Above them, in the little village by the sea, the children are learning carols to sing at Easter, and every day the sky and water are growing bluer.

The root girls take their dresses to show to the good Earth Mother, where she sits comfortably with her tea and her knitting. Her busy ant helpers are about her. She is pleased when she sees how well each little root girl has made her Spring dress.

It is time to be ready, for above them the ice on the little brook has melted and the water is slipping merrily over its pebbles. In the barns the sheep and lambs feel the Spring air and wish to be in the green fields again.

While the little root girls are sewing Spring dresses, the root boys are busy with their share in making ready for Spring. They wake up the sleeping insects — the beetles, grasshoppers, ladybirds, crickets, bumble-bees, fireflies and June-bugs. They sponge them and paint their shells with bright

Spring colours, while the fields over their heads are growing greener and the leaf-buds on the trees are swelling in the warm Spring air.

Then, when all is ready, Spring comes!

First the meadow grasses fan out over the countryside, green and lovely, waving in the wind.

Then come the busy insects, eager to do their work in fields and woods and gardens, singing and humming and leaping.

Next the good grains push their heads above the ground.

Last, and most beautiful of all, the flowers parade in a sweet and gay procession — snowdrop and star-grass, forget-me-not and violet, dandelion, columbine, daisy and primrose; liverwort, lily, anemone and poppy, cornflower, clover and bluebell.

Out they troop joyfully, out of their earth home into the lovely world, where birds fly in the blue sky above the green meadows.

The root children scatter far and wide. Some choose the deep woods and, as lilies-of-the valley and violets, bloom shyly under the trees. Gay butterflies hover above them, scarlet toadstools brighten the moss, and the slow snail creeps out of his house, glad that Spring has come again.

Others hurry to the pond-side and play there all day long, making it gay with water-lilies, forget-me-nots and wild iris. Spiders spin lovely webs that shine in the sun. The reeds wave and rustle in the passing wind, and dragon-flies dart hither and thither.

Still others play in the meadows, dancing merrily under the sunny sky with the beetles and butterflies, to the music of grasshoppers' chirping, the bees' humming. Each little root girl is now a poppy or a daisy, a bluebell or a cornflower, or a graceful yarrow flower.

And so they play all Summer long, until a day comes when the air is chill and the leaves, turned red and gold and brown, are fluttering down to earth. The root children come running over the hills and valleys, from meadows, woods and brookside, back to the Earth Mother, who welcomes them to their warm earth home to rest and sleep the cold winter through, until Spring comes again next year!

Adapted from a story by Sibylle V. Olfers and Helen Dean Fish

Legend of the Tree and the Cross

When Adam and Eve disobeyed the Lord God and ate from the tree which gave knowledge of good and evil, God sent them out of the Garden of Eden. He set Cherubim with flaming swords to keep Adam and Eve from returning to Paradise to eat from the Tree of Eternal Life as well.

Many years passed. Life on earth was hard for Adam and Eve. Yet great joy filled them when they remembered how they had walked and talked with the Lord God in the beautiful Garden of Eden, amid the trees. And they often told their children and grandchildren stories about Paradise.

When Adam was very old and ill, he sent his son Seth to the Gates of Paradise to ask God for oil from the Tree of Mercy to ease his pain.

The Archangel Michael met Seth at the Gates. "I cannot give you what you seek," he said. "Only Christ, the merciful Son of God, can bring the Oil of Mercy to man; and several thousand years are needed to prepare His coming. However," the Archangel continued, "so that your father Adam may help the Son of God bring this Oil of Mercy to mankind, I will give you three seeds from the Tree of Life."

Seth returned home, and when Adam died, Seth planted the three seeds upon his grave. From the seeds three saplings grew and merged into one great tree trunk.

Many sacred things were made from the wood of the tree, including the rod used by Moses. Later, after the tree was cut down, it was used over a doorway in Solomon's Temple. Still later, part of the tree became a bridge over which Jesus walked on his way to be crucified. And part of the tree was used as the cross itself, from which Jesus Christ poured forth both mercy and life into the earth, blessing all mankind and giving the promise of Eternal Life to all who will receive it.

The Feast of Eostre

Gunther was a young Saxon boy who lived many years ago in Germany. One morning his eyes shone with excitement as he quickly ate his breakfast of barley bread and goat's cheese.

"I'm going to look for ducks' eggs today, Mother, and I will make some clay eggs as well," he said.

"Good!" said his mother. "The day after tomorrow is the first day of spring and the Goddess Eostre must be honoured with a feast of eggs — for they are the symbol of new life! And Gunther —," his mother continued, "this year you may roll the eggs over the barley field by yourself."

"Oh, Mother, thank you!" cried Gunther. "I will do it well, I promise." He felt suddenly very proud and grown up.

Rolling the eggs over the fields was an important task; it was part of Gunther's religion, and his people believed it would make the earth fertile. Each year at the Feast of Eostre, they rolled coloured eggs where they intended to plant grain to make certain they would have a good crop.

Gunther kissed his mother goodbye and ran from their thatched hut to the nearby marshes. There he searched among the reeds until he spied a nest full of duck's eggs. Carefully he tucked the eggs into the folds of his deerskin tunic and carried them home.

"Splendid," cried his mother, "I shall cook them at once."

After the eggs had been boiled in an earthen pot, Gunther painted them red; for the Saxons believed that the colour red brought good fortune.

Next day, as Gunther proudly rolled the painted eggs over the barley field, he took special care to look for places where hares nested.

"Did you hide the eggs well?" asked Gunther's mother on his return home. "If the witches get them, the Goddess will be very angry with us!"

"Don't worry, Mother," answered Gunther, "I hid half of them in a hare's nest by the fallen oak tree, and half in a nest in the centre of the field."

"Good!" said his mother. "The witches may find out where you hid them, but the hares will protect them. They are the sacred animals of the Goddess Eostre." Then, patting Gunther's shoulder, she added with pride, "You have done well, my son. We shall surely have a splendid barley crop. And tomorrow, with the other boys and girls, you can collect the eggs again for the Feast of Eostre."

That was the Spring Festival in Germany, two thousand years ago, when there had never yet been a Christian Easter. Gunther's great-grandchildren, however, in their eagerness to receive the new life-giving message of Love that Christianity brought to their land, forgot about the Goddess Eostre. But they never forgot the joyful custom of colouring eggs in springtime. The story of the hare, too, has come down through the ages; and even the word Eostre remains. It has merely been changed in spelling to Easter!

Abridged from a story by Martha Knapp

83

A Lesson of Faith

"Please help me. I need someone to care for my children!" cried a beautiful, delicate Butterfly to a pudgy, green Caterpillar who was strolling along a cabbage leaf in her odd lumbering way. "I am dying," continued the Butterfly, "but look! Here on this cabbage leaf are my little eggs. Oh, who will feed and care for my baby Butterflies after they are born? Will you please, gentle green Caterpillar? Oh, oh! How dizzy I am!"

And with these words the Butterfly drooped her wings and died; and the green Caterpillar was left standing alone by the side of the Butterfly's eggs. "She has chosen *me*?" exclaimed the Caterpillar. "A poor crawling creature like me to bring up her dainty little ones!"

However, the green Caterpillar had a kind heart, so she resolved to do her best. "But I don't even know what to feed baby Butterflies." she exclaimed. And so then and there she decided to consult her wise friend, the Lark. "He knows many things," she thought, "because he flies so very high!" For to fly up into the sky (which she could never do) was the Caterpillar's idea of perfect glory.

So she told the Lark all her difficulties and begged him to find out how she was to feed the little Butterfly babies — so different from herself!

The next day the Lark returned. "I've news! Wonderful news!" sang the Lark. "But you probably won't believe me!"

"Oh yes, I believe everything I'm told," said the Caterpillar.

"Well then," said the Lark, "first of all, can you guess what these little creatures are to eat when they hatch?"

"Why, dew and honey from flowers," sighed the Caterpillar.

"No such thing, my dear," trilled the Lark. "You are to feed them the same cabbage leaves that you eat!"

"Never!" cried the Caterpillar indignantly. "That is impossible! You must be mistaken!"

"I warned you that you wouldn't believe me!" said the Lark. "But listen, dear Caterpillar. What do you think those little eggs will turn out to be?"

"Why, Butterflies, of course," replied the Caterpillar.

"No! They will be Caterpillars!" declared the Lark.

"What nonsense!" cried the pudgy green Caterpillar. "And I thought you were so wise!"

"Oh dear", sighed the Lark. "I'm afraid you have neither faith nor trust. And I have so much more to tell you. If only you would believe me."

"I believe everything I'm told," repeated the Caterpillar again, with as grave a face as if it were a fact.

"Oh, I hope so," sang the Lark, "for here's the best news of all! You, you pudgy green Caterpillar, will one day be a Butterfly yourself!"

"Wretched bird, go away! Now you make cruel jokes!" cried the Caterpillar. "That is impossible!"

"Oh, Caterpillar," said the Lark gently, "when I fly high in the sky I see so many wonderful things! It is only because you crawl along and never get beyond your cabbage-leaf that you call anything impossible!"

At that the Caterpillar wept. "Look at my long, pudgy, green body and these endless legs — how could I ever be a dainty, winged Butterfly?"

"But you will be!" Have faith in the future!" sang the Lark.

"But how am I to learn faith?" asked the Caterpillar.

At that moment she felt a movement at her side. She looked around — and there — eight or ten little fuzzy Caterpillars were moving about. They had broken free from the Butterfly's eggs and were already munching on the cabbage-leaf.

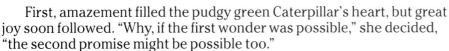

First, amazement filled the pudgy green Caterpillar's heart, but great joy soon followed. "Why, if the first wonder was possible," she decided, "the second promise might be possible too."

"Oh, please teach me your lessons, Lark!" she called out. And the joyful Lark spoke to her of the wonders on the earth and of the heaven above.

The green Caterpillar talked to her friends and relatives, during all the rest of her life, of the time when she would become a Butterfly. But not one of them believed her! Nevertheless, she had learned the Lark's lesson of faith, and as she entered into her chrysalis grave, she said, "I shall become a Butterfly!"

And when she did become a Butterfly, she flew high, high in the sky and looked upon the beauty of the world. And when it was time for her to die again, she said —

"I have known so many wonders — I have faith — I now can trust what shall come next!"

Adapted from a story by Margaret Gatty

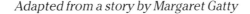

The Raising of Lazarus

And Jesus lifted up his eyes, and said, Father, I thank thee that thou has heard me. And when he had thus spoken, he cried with a loud voice, Lazarus come forth. And he that was dead came forth, bound hand and foot with graveclothes.

John 11:41b, 43, 44a

One day when Jesus was with His disciples, he learned that His beloved Lazarus was dying. Jesus travelled to the home of Lazarus, in Bethany. When He arrived he was told that Lazarus had died four days earlier and that his body had already been placed in a tomb. Martha and Mary, the grieving sisters of Lazarus, took Jesus to the tomb, and Jesus said to them, "Your brother shall rise again." Then Jesus told the people of Bethany, who gathered around, to take away the large stone that sealed the tomb. After praying to God, His Father, Jesus called out, "Lazarus, come forth!" Lazarus came back to life and stepped out of the tomb.

Through this great miracle, many people came to believe in Jesus as the Messiah — so many that the Pharisees and the ruling priests of the Jews became deeply afraid. They said, "This man performs so many miracles that unless we stop Him, all men will believe in Him. They will try to make him King. The Romans will never allow that, and they will make war upon us and destroy our nation and our people." And from that day, the ruling priests plotted against Jesus.

Passover

And the Jews' Passover was nigh at hand: and many went out of the country up to Jerusalem . . ."

John 11:55

The Hebrew word for Passover is *Pesach*, and in many European languages the name for Easter come from this word. The French word for Easter is *Paques;* the Spanish, *Pascua;* the Greek, *Pascha;* the Norwegian, *Paaske;* the Italian, *Pasqua.*

Originally celebrated as a joyous spring festival which welcomes the revival of nature from its winter sleep, Passover has another and better known meaning. It is the Jewish Festival of Freedom. The Book of Exodus gives us the story.

Hundreds of years before the coming of Jesus, many of the people of Israel lived in Egypt — as slaves. At last the Lord God sent Moses to lead the Jews out of Egypt. But Pharaoh, the King of the Egyptians, would not allow them to leave. The Lord God sent many trials and plagues to the Egyptian people, but still Pharaoh would not let the Children of Israel go. Finally, God sent the Angel of Death to take away the first-born in each of the Egyptian houses, including Pharaoh's own son and heir. But the Angel of Death 'passed over' the houses of the Hebrews. Only then did Pharaoh allow the Jews to leave Egypt; and led by Moses, they found freedom. The Lord God then commanded that each year, from the fourteenth day of the Hebrew month of *Nisan** until the twenty-first day of *Nisan,* the Children of Israel should celebrate the Passover.

**In the Jewish lunar calendar, the fourteenth day of Nisan can fall anywhere between March 22 and April 22.*

Holy Week

The last week of Lent is Holy Week. It recalls the events of Jesus Christ's last week on earth.

Palm Sunday

The first day of Holy Week is Palm Sunday. Its name is taken from the palm branches with which the people welcomed Jesus as He made His entry into Jerusalem. At that time, making a carpet of palms and waving palm branches was the accepted way of welcoming a hero.

Many of the people who cheered Jesus and called Him 'King', wanted Him to be their earthly king and free them from the rule of the Romans. But Jesus was teaching about His Kingdom, the Kingdom of God. His power was inner power. He sent His disciples to bring Him a humble donkey colt and on this He rode into Jerusalem.

Dear donkey with your shaggy coat
He asked for *you*, not a horse or a goat!
For he knew that by you he'd not be failed
On that Day of Palms when as 'King' He was hailed.
Two disciples he sent to that village small —
To fetch you. He said — and the Gospels recall —
"If anyone asks, say 'The Lord has need
Of a donkey colt to be His steed'."
Oh, donkey with your hide so tough,
He stroked your coat so soft, yet rough,
Before you started along the track
With the Son of Man upon your back.
For He'd chosen *you* for that fateful ride
To the city where He would be *Glorified!*

Monday and Tuesday of Holy Week

On these two days, Jesus went to the Holy Temple in Jerusalem to teach. On the first Monday morning, in the Temple Courtyard, He found the money-changers and merchants selling sacrificial doves at high prices. He overturned their tables and as He threw them out, He said, "It is written in the scriptures, 'My Temple is to be a house of prayer' — but you have turned it into a den of robbers!"

Then Jesus began to teach the crowds who gathered around Him. Some men tried to trick Jesus into speaking against the Roman Government or into saying that He was the King of the Jews. If He had done so, He could legally have been accused of treason or blasphemy. But Jesus could not be tricked, and He answered all their questions with wisdom.

On these two days He also told His disciples about many things that would happen in the future and that He would be seen again, coming in the clouds of heaven with power and great glory.

Wednesday of Holy Week

This is believed to have been a day of quiet for Jesus. Surrounded by His close friends in Bethany, He prepared Himself for what He knew was to come. This is also the day when Judas Iscariot betrayed Jesus to the chief priests of the Temple.

Maundy Thursday

'Maundy' is believed to have come from a Latin word meaning 'commandment'. On this day, at His Last Supper, Jesus said to His disciples, "A new commandment I give to you — that you Love one another as I have loved you."

During this Last Supper, Jesus also shared bread with the disciples and said, "Do this in memory of me — for this is my body which will be given for you." Then He shared a cup of wine with them and said, "This is my blood which will be shed for many." Many Christian churches celebrate this as the sacrament of Holy Communion.

At His Last Supper, Jesus also washed the feet of His disciples and said, "You ought also to wash one another's feet."

Through the ages Christians have tried to follow the example set by Jesus. Even kings and queens used to wash the feet of some of their subjects on Maundy Thursday. Later, the custom arose of giving Maundy Money to the poor, which still takes place each year in Britain.

Maundy Thursday was also known as 'Pure' or 'Clean' Thursday for it was on this day that people bathed and cleansed themselves in preparation for Easter.

Good Friday

The Friday before Easter is known as 'Good Friday'. Our English word, good, comes from the word 'God', and originally this day was probably called 'God's Friday'. It is celebrated by millions of Christians as the day of mourning for Christ's suffering and His death upon the cross.

In many cities around the world, there are processions through the streets on this day. One of the oldest of these processions is in Jerusalem. Every year pilgrims from all over the world, singing and carrying heavy crosses, walk up the *Via Dolorosa* to the Church of the Holy Sepulchre. This is the path which Jesus is believed to have travelled, carrying His cross. Around the world, many churches hold services between noon and three o'clock in the afternoon. This is accepted as the time that Jesus was on the cross.

In Seville, Spain, and in Mexico, Monaco, Italy, South America and in many other countries, colourful processions are held in which beautifully carved or decorated figures, representing the chief characters of the Passion Week, are mounted on platforms and carried through the streets. One particularly moving moment often portrayed is from the Gospel of John, when Mary, the Mother of Jesus, stood before the cross. Beside her was John, the disciple whom Jesus loved best. Jesus wanted His mother to be well cared for. From the cross He said to her, as He looked toward John, "Woman, behold your son." And to John He said, "Behold your mother." From that day, John took Mary into his home and cared for her as though she were his own mother.

To the early Christians it seemed that all of nature, the earth, and her plants and animals shared in the joy or sorrow of God's Son. Many legends sprang up telling of their devotion to Jesus. This one comes from Ireland.

The Robin and the Thorns

It had grown quite dark on that fateful day, although it was still mid-afternoon. The air was hot and stifling and even the little brown robin who came flying to the hill near Jerusalem could scarcely breathe.

As the robin came to Calvary it saw Jesus upon the cross. The bird flew closer and saw the crown of thorns upon Jesus' head. One of the thorns had pierced the skin of Christ's forehead and the robin flew down and plucked out the thorn. As it did, a drop of Christ's blood from His wound fell upon the robin's little breast. And from that time, the legend tells, the breasts of all robins are red, as a reminder that one of them tried to ease the suffering of our Lord.

Holy Saturday

A great hush had fallen over the city of Jerusalem on that Saturday so long ago. It was the Jewish Sabbath, when no work was allowed. The friends and disciples of Jesus as well as His mother, Mary, were filled with grief. They felt lost and bewildered. Although Jesus had told them that He would rise from the dead, not one of them believed that such a thing was possible.

On Saturday night many of the followers of Jesus waited impatiently. They longed to go to Jesus' burial place and to be near their Lord — even to His lifeless body! At last they could wait no longer. In the early hours of the morning, while it was still dark, small groups of those who loved Jesus began to make their way to His tomb.

From earliest Christian times, Easter Eve has been celebrated as a period of vigil — of watching and waiting for the Resurrection. It was often celebrated by lighting bonfires or Paschal candles. In many countries lighted candles are carried through the streets. At the beginning of some Easter Eve services the church is in darkness. Then each member of the congregation lights a small candle from one large Paschal candle. Soon the whole church is blazing with light.

Easter Sunday

He is not here; for he is risen . . .
     Matthew 28:6a

*. . . Be not affrighted: Ye seek Jesus of
Nazareth which was crucified; he is risen;
he is not here . . .*
        Mark 16:6

*Why seek ye the living among the dead?
He is not here, but is risen . . .*
      Luke 24:5b-6a

*For as yet they did not know the scripture,
that he must rise again from the dead.*
       John 20:9

Early on Sunday morning while it was still dark, Mary Magdalene, one of the women who loved Jesus very much, went to His tomb. To her amazement, she saw that the great stone which sealed the entrance had been rolled aside. The tomb was empty!

Mary ran to find John and Peter. "They have taken away the Lord and I don't know where they have put His body," she cried.

John and Peter ran to the tomb. They went inside. The linen burial clothes were there — but the Lord's body was gone!

After the disciples went away, Mary Magdalene remained outside the tomb, weeping. All at once she saw a man standing nearby. It was Jesus. But Mary did not recognise Him. Jesus spoke to her, "Woman, why are you crying? Whom are you seeking?" Still Mary did not recognise Him. She thought He must be the gardener.

Jesus came closer. Gently He called her by name, "Mary . . ." That was all He said, but with that utterance of her name, her eyes were opened. She knew that Jesus was alive again!

"Master!" she cried, her whole being flooded with joy!

"Find my brothers," Jesus said. "Tell them that I go now to my Father and your Father; to My God and your God."

When Jesus had gone, a radiant Mary hurried to the disciples. "I have seen the Lord," she cried. "The Master lives!"

That same evening the disciples and friends of Jesus were gathered together. Other followers besides Mary Magdalene had seen the Risen Christ during the day. Several of the women had seen Him, and Cleopas and Simon had been with Him in the village of Emmaus. All of these witnesses told their stories. Over and over they repeated that they had seen Jesus; that He was *alive!* But most of the disciples could not believe it.

Suddenly, although all the doors were bolted, Jesus appeared in their midst! The disciples were frightened and bewildered. Was it an Angel they were seeing? Was it a spirit?

Jesus spoke to them, "Peace be with you." He showed them the wounds on His hands and feet. "Touch me and see for yourselves," He said. "A spirit does not have flesh and bones as I have."

At last the disciples no longer doubted that Jesus Christ was risen. They knew He was alive and their joy was wonderful to behold.

For the next forty days the Risen Christ taught His beloved disciples before He sent them forth to tell the world that *Easter Day was only the beginning.*

Eastertide

From Easter to Ascension

But Easter is not over, in fact it's just begun,
For now the Resurrection by each man must be won.

Easter Is

Easter is a happy time
When birdsongs fill the air,
When childish laughter, light and gay,
Is ringing everywhere.

Easter is a joyous time,
So let your voice be heard
In joyful alleluias
To Christ, the risen Lord.

Easter's Resurrection time,
And let us not forget,
That He who rose up from the grave
Is living with us yet.

Easter is so many things,
All lovely to behold,
To cherish in fond memory
To guard, and to enfold.

Selections from 'Easter Is' by Mrs. Paul E. King

The Legend of Thomas and the Iris

Thomas had not been with the other disciples when Jesus appeared to them on Easter night — and when the others told Thomas that Jesus Christ had risen from the dead, he refused to believe it.

The following day, as he was walking outside the city of Jerusalem, Thomas saw by the roadside the lovely purple blossoms of iris plants. As he stopped to admire their beauty, he recalled that only a few days before, he had seen these same plants, brown and withered. Thomas had been certain that the plants were dead. Now they were radiant with life! In that moment his mind became open, belief began to grow and hope entered his heart. The little iris had helped him remember that with God, all things are possible. Soon after, the Risen Jesus appeared to Thomas.

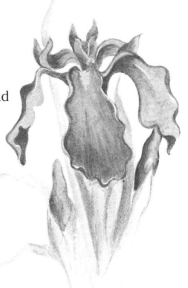

A Thought for all Seasons

Because of His boundless love
He became what we are
In order that
He might make us what He is.

Irenaeus (c. 130 to 200 A.D.)

The Maid of Emmaus

It was Passover week, and another long, hard day at the Inn in Emmaus. From early morning Martha, the orphaned servant girl, had rushed from here to there, under the sharp commands and stinging blows of old Jonas and his shrewish wife, Sarah.

Passover week was especially busy at the Inn, serving the many travellers who stopped on their way to Jerusalem. But this week, in spite of the long days and frequent blows, Martha moved as if in a happy dream; for she, too, was planning a pilgrimage.

Only the week before she had been sent on an errand to Jerusalem. There in the courtyard of the Holy Temple, Martha had met the Master. Enraptured by the infinite tenderness of His gaze she had listened to Him teach. Then Jesus had called to her by name and said that she, too, would be His disciple! For Martha, nothing in the world would ever be the same!

On her return to Emmaus, one thought carried her forward — to take Him a gift, to show Him how much she loved Him. Slowly an idea came. She would bake bread for Him — perfect loaves of bread, made from the finest wheat. She would take them to the Master in Jerusalem as soon as the Passover was over. If *only* she could find a way to purchase the costly wheat!

Now, as Martha swept the courtyard at the Inn, the answer came. She remembered the gold chain which had belonged to her mother. Dear as it was to her, no sacrifice was too great to show Jesus her love for Him.

Next day Martha traded her gold chain for wheat — the finest wheat, which made flour that was white as snow!

On the morning after Passover had ended, while Sarah and Jonas slept, Martha rose two hours before dawn. Trembling in fear of discovery, she mixed the dough and baked the bread — four perfect loaves!

Just as the sun crept over the hills, Martha fled from the Inn, carrying her precious basket of bread. Her feet seemed almost to fly over the road to Jerusalem. "Never", she thought, "has there been such a glorious morning."

But when she arrived at the city, she could not find the Master at the Holy Temple. Anxiously she approached a gentle-looking woman who was passing by. "Have you seen the Master, Jesus" she asked timidly, "the one who is called the Christ?"

Quickly the woman drew Martha into the shadow of a wall. "Oh, child," she whispered fearfully, "have you not heard! Do you not know that He was crucified three days ago!"

A single cry of pain escaped Martha's lips. The world began to spin around her. She slumped against the wall and would have fallen had the woman not come to her aid.

The woman took Martha to a secluded spot nearby. There, as gently as possible, she told Martha the story of that terrible Friday past. "So many of us trusted that He was the Redeemer of Israel," she said. "Some say that today He is alive again, risen; but it can only be an idle tale. For I saw Him die on the cross!"

For Martha, the road back to Emmaus seemed endless. Hopelessly she stumbled on and on as the words kept ringing in her ears, "Dead, crucified!" How could it be?

It was late afternoon when she reached Emmaus, still clutching the basket of bread. As she was about to enter the Inn she suddenly turned aside. "No," she thought, quickly hiding the basket, "I will never surrender *His* bread to Jonas and Sarah." As she entered the Inn, the blows from Jonas came as she had known they would. She had no strength to resist the savage beating. For a long time she lay where she had fallen, beside the oven — the oven where only at day-break she had laboured in ecstasy.

Martha was aroused by men's voices from outside the Inn. She recognized one of them as Cleopas, a kind man who always stopped at the Inn on his trips to and from Jerusalem.

"Stay here with us," she heard Cleopas say, "for the day is far spent."

Three men entered the Inn, Cleopas, a man he called Simon, and another — a stranger whose face she could not see.

Martha had risen with infinite pain and Cleopas greeted her kindly. She set about placing food upon the table — barley cakes and oil, wine and raisins. "Such a meagre meal for weary travellers," she thought, and then, something about the presence of the three men touched her. She felt strangely soothed and protected by their presence. Impulsively she slipped out of the Inn.

A moment later she returned carrying her four loaves of bread which she quickly placed on the table. Her eyes, dim with tears, watched the loaves as they lay there, snowy and fair. The longing in her heart, the treasured gold chain, the swelling bruises of her poor beaten body; all these had helped to purchase them. At that moment she raised her eyes and her glance rested on the face of the stranger. Then she cried out!

Why, he was *not* a stranger! His eyes! It was as though all the colour of the sunset and all the radiance of the dawn were behind His eyes — shining, majestic and glorified, yet filled with compassion and love.

He was gazing steadfastly upon her loaves of bread. He reached forward and touched them, broke them and held them out. And as He raised His eyes to Heaven — a blinding radiance of glory surrounded Him.

Cleopas and Simon leaned forward, breathless, transfixed. Martha crept closer and knelt within the circle of light.

"Master," she tried to whisper, "Master . . ."

Jesus turned then, to look at her. There was no need for her to speak. He knew. He understood. Gently His healing radiance enfolded her.

Then as softly as the sunset goes, the celestial light died away. The Master's chair was empty.

Cleopas and Simon sat spellbound, gazing at the place where the spendour had been. Martha still knelt in a rapture of joy and peace.

On the table lay the little loaves, uneaten, but received and blessed.

Agnes Sligh Turnbull

93

The Days After Easter

In many countries Easter Monday and Tuesday, the two days *after* Easter, are celebrated as holidays. Banks and government offices are closed and children enjoy a holiday from school. When the weather is good, families join together on outings to the countryside or visit the city parks. In England, the colourful Easter Monday Parade draws crowds of eager spectators to London's Battersea Park.

Most of the early customs of Easter Monday and Tuesday have been forgotten, but some are celebrated in parts of Europe even to this day. In country villages, boys and girls enjoy the custom of 'drenching' or 'dousing' and splash each other with bottles or buckets of water. Water is an important religious symbol for washing away old faults and bad habits so that they may be replaced with new abilities. The ancient custom of 'switching' also survives, as children and grown-ups gently tap each other with slender green branches to give 'a stroke of health'. In many countries people exchange brightly coloured and decorated eggs as a token of the Resurrection. In some eastern countries the traditional greeting is "Christ is risen," which is answered by "Truly He is risen!" — a wonderful reminder of the original meaning of 'The Days After Easter'.

In the United States, although Easter Monday and Tuesday are not recognised as legal or school holidays, a grand egg-rolling party is given by the President and the First Lady of the United States on Easter Monday. Every year, hundreds of children roll eggs down the grassy slopes of the White House lawn in Washington. There are musical bands and many prizes and gifts for the running and tumbling children. Their happy shouts ring out the message that Easter celebrations are a joyful part of our lives!

The Great Easter Egg Dilemma of 1877!

Fanny and Scott Hayes loved living in the White House where their father, Rutherford B. Hayes, had just become President of the United States. Eagerly the children looked forward to the traditional Easter egg-rolling in the grounds of the Capitol Building in Washington, D.C.

Dolly Madison, wife of President James Madison, had begun the Easter Monday egg-rolling in 1814. Every year hundreds of children each brought a basket of gaily painted eggs to compete in rolling them down the Capitol slopes — hopefully to finish unbroken! But then came the great Easter Egg dilemma of 1877! A new lawn had been planted on the Capitol slopes. The gardeners cancelled the egg-rolling!

Fanny Hayes pleaded with her father, "Please, can't you do anything? You're the President of the United States!" And the President tried, but still the gardeners refused. Then Mrs. Hayes spoke up, "Rutherford, we cannot disappoint all those children! Let's have the Easter egg-rolling right here on the White House lawn." The President agreed, and so, to this day, each President and his family invite hundreds of children to the White House lawn egg-rolling on the Monday after Easter!

The Welcome

A Slavonic Easter Legend

It was Easter Sunday more than a thousand years ago, in a small Slavic village. Although the villagers had recently become Christians, their feelings for the old gods were still strong. Now, following the Easter Service, they listened as the village story-teller told the legend of how the old gods welcomed the Saviour.

"It was still dark on that first Easter morning when the Saviour, Isus Hristos, rose from the dead. When He stepped forth from the grave, He was only as big as a man; but with each step He took, He grew bigger. When He reached the forests, He had become tall as the fir trees. When He came to the mountains, His head towered above them all.

"As He travelled across other lands and seas, the lofty old gods and goddesses of the different peoples of the earth came forth to see Him. They had all been watching Him, fearful that He might not rise and come forth. Isus Hristos walked on. And all the gods followed until He reached our lands. Then the gods of the Slavs began to speak:

"'I am like the sun' said Svetovit-the-great. 'I melt the snow in the spring. I ripen men's corn in summer. I am the flame in the fire. I can burn gently or grow fierce and burn up whole villages!'

"Then the thunder-god said, 'I send the lightning which purifies the sky and the rain that nourishes the dry earth.'

"And then Zeus spoke up and all the other old gods agreed, 'Every one of us has power. Men and the earth need us to survive. Not one of us gods would allow men to crucify us! Show us why you did, Isus Hristos. Show us what powers you bring to earth and to men!'

"Before the eyes of all the old gods, the Saviour began to grow, spreading out over the whole earth; rising above the clouds and up to the stars. The crown of thorns dropped from the Saviour's head and where it fell on to the earth, a forest sprang forth. From the cruel wounds on His hands and feet, streams of milk and honey flowed into the earth. And from the wounds in the Saviour's side, streams of light and warmth rayed forth. All the earth became greener, and the waters more living, and the earth and the plants, the rivers and the seas — even the clouds — sang out in a chorus: *'THE LORD IS RISEN!'*

"The Saviour then raised His hands in blessing and each man and woman began to shine with new inner light! With awe the old gods watched this happen and together they too sang out: *'THE LORD IS RISEN!'*

"'Isus Hristos, oh, great and mighty Spirit!' cried all the gods. 'Now we believe that you are the Creator. We are but sparks emerging from your staff ready to serve you'.

"Then Svetovit and all the strong gods and goddesses surrounded the Saviour with fiery tongues of flame. And all the gentle gods and goddesses surrounded His head with bright and shining stars.

"For Isus Hristos is the true, the only God!" said the story-teller ecstatically, as he finished his story. "He is like the sea from which all rivers emerge and to which all rivers return. *HE IS!*"

Then a great glad song burst from all the people of the small Slavic village: "The Lord is risen!" they sang. "Truly He is risen! *HE IS EVERYWHERE!*"

Forty Days with the Risen Christ

Jesus was alive! His followers and friends had seen Him die — now He was alive again! At times they could see Him, embrace Him and feel the bliss of His presence. At other times they searched but could not find Him. Jesus could appear among His followers quite suddenly, in spite of locked doors and windows; for His body was different since His Resurrection.

For forty days, beginning with Easter Sunday, the Risen Christ came to His disciples, strengthening them, teaching them many hidden meanings of the scriptures and secrets of the Kingdom of God.

The Bible tells little of Christ's teachings and deeds during those forty days; however, the Gospel of John relates: "And there are also many other things which Jesus did, the which, if they should be written every one, I suppose that even the world itself could not contain the books that should be written."*

*John 21 : 25

With Jesus on the Sea of Galilee

The night was clear. A thousand stars glistened in the sky and the peaceful waters of the Sea of Galilee were streaked with a silver sheen from the light of the waning moon. In an open fishing boat, rocked by the gentle motion of the water, the disciples lay sleeping.

On Easter Sunday, after the Resurrection, the disciples had been told that Jesus would meet them in Galilee, but He had not yet appeared. And when night came, Peter, John and Thomas, along with several other disciples, had come out onto the lake to fish, casting their nets into the moonlit water before falling asleep.

When they awakened, the morning mist surrounded them and, as they pulled up their nets, they found they had not caught even a single fish. Disappointed, the disciples looked up just as the newly risen sun, like a bright orb, began to burn through the mist. They saw a man standing on the shore, at the water's edge. The man called out to them, "Cast your nets on the *right* side of the boat and you will find fish."

They did as the man instructed. Soon the disciples pulled in their nets. It was like a miracle. They had caught so many fish they could not lift up the nets!

Looking again to the man on shore, John had a sudden flash of inspiration. "It is the Lord!" he cried.

When the disciples reached the shore, Jesus was waiting for them. He had built a fire and together they cooked fish. And the Risen Jesus gave bread and fish to each of the disciples and ate with them. It was like a glorious dream. Then Jesus said to Peter, "Feed my lambs. Feed my sheep," and all the disciples understood that Jesus had a great work for them to do — for, the whole world waited to hear the message that only they could bring — the message of the Risen Christ.

Ascensiontide

The Ten Days between Ascension and Whitsun

> In heavy clouds let Him be drawn
> And so let Him be downward borne.
> In cooling streams let Him be sent,
> In flames and fire blaze His descent.
> In air and essence, sound and dew,
> To permeate our whole earth through.
>
> *Novalis*

On the fortieth day after Easter, the Risen Jesus led His disciples, together with five hundred other followers, to the Mount of Olives near Jerusalem. There, on the hillside, under the warmth of the springtime sun, amidst the budding and blossoming of flowers, Jesus spoke to His disciples. He told them to wait in Jerusalem until they received a new kind of Baptism — the Baptism of the Holy Spirit which would come soon. With love shining from His eyes, Jesus blessed all His followers. "Lo, I am with you always, even unto the end of the world," He promised. Then, before their very eyes, Jesus began to ascend. The Bible relates that 'a cloud received Him'. No longer were his followers able to see Him.

The day that this occurred is celebrated as Ascension Day. It always falls on a Thursday, on the fortieth day after Easter Sunday. 'Ascension' means 'going up' and when we say that Jesus 'ascended to Heaven', we must remember that 'ascending' may also mean moving on to a higher level or to a different state of being. On Ascension Day, Jesus Christ entered into another, higher condition or 'way' of being. This is one of the great *mysteries* of Christianity.

The Bible draws our attention to the clouds and to that wonderful cycle of rising and falling, when moisture is drawn up into the sky, becoming visible as a cloud, then falling again as rain. Jesus Christ is often referred to as 'Lord of the Elements' and all four elements, earth, air, water and fire (warmth) are needed to form the ever-changing kingdom of the clouds which moves between the heavens and the earth.

The Second Coming of Christ

As the followers of Jesus stood gazing up towards the heavens on that first Ascension Day, the Bible tells that two Angels appeared and told them that as Jesus had been received into the clouds, so 'in like manner' He would come again*.

Jesus, before His death and Resurrection, had also told His disciples that He would some day come again and that He would be seen coming in the clouds of heaven with power and great glory**. This is known as the 'Second Coming of Christ'. Christianity teaches that although Jesus Christ is always with us, He is hidden from our physical sight, as if by clouds. It teaches that Christ will come again — that we will be able to see Him clearly once more.

Some Christians believe that He will come again in a physical body, as He did nearly two thousand years ago. Other Christians believe that he will be seen only in His Resurrected body, able to appear and disappear at will. Still other Christians believe that men and women must strengthen their own powers of love, thought, faith and of their inner sight, so that they can see through the 'cloud covering' which surrounds Christ. When many people have been able to do this, they believe that all mankind will then be able to see and experience Christ.

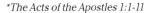

*The Acts of the Apostles 1:1-11
**Matthew 24:30

Aqua and Her Sisters

Once there was — in the future there will be, and now, there is — a little raindrop which we may name 'Aqua'.

Now Aqua has many sister-raindrops and together they often visit our earth. Aqua leads a very interesting life. Often she is high up in the clouds which always change their forms and dissolve and drift between heaven and earth. When she is in the clouds, she is so fine and delicate and dissolved that she seems to be everywhere in the whole cloud all at the same time. Aqua feels that she is one with the cloud, all of it, and that it is her home. She loves all that comes to her from above — the light and the warmth of the sun and the glow and shimmer of the stars. Yet Aqua and her sisters also truly love the earth. Whenever tiny specks of dust drift up from the earth, Aqua and her sisters lovingly enfold them with their moisture. Droplets of water form. Soon they become heavier and heavier until eagerly they travel down, down, down to earth.

As the droplets splash onto the earth they sing a merry little tune, "Plip, plip, pitter, patter, splish, splash," as though to tell how happy they are to be back again. For here on earth, Aqua and all her sisters become part of all living things. Not only people and animals and plants need them for life itself, but even the hard and beautifully shaped crystals need them in order to build their lovely forms.

When Aqua and her sisters come to earth they often form puddles and ponds, rivers and lakes and, yes, even oceans. They help to feed and to make everything grow. Sometimes Aqua and her sisters stay for only a few months in the grain, sometimes some will stay for a lifetime in a big tree. But when Aqua and her sisters become free again, they will rise once more, following the warm sunbeams back up, up, up into the clouds which form and drift between heaven and earth.

Wherever Aqua and her sisters may be, and no matter in what form, as raindrops, snowflakes or hailstones; as sparkling dew, morning mist or evening fog, whether they are part of the rainbow or floating in a cloud, God's Angels are there too, helping to build up life and to make new forms.

And so, as people walk out-of-doors on Ascension Day, as they watch the clouds overhead, and look to see the changes that have come about in nature since Easter Sunday, they give thanks to God for Aqua and her sisters. They give thanks for the precious gift of water and for the realm of the clouds — God's misty bridge between heaven and earth.

Adapted from the story, 'Aqua — the Raindrop' by Richard H. Lewis

Well-Dressing at Tissington

It was Ascension Day, and long before dawn Jenny and her father hurried through the streets of Tissington, a small English village in Derbyshire. Jenny's eyes danced with excitement for in a moment they would join other villagers to add the finishing touches to the beautiful floral mosaics that would decorate the five ancient wells of Tissington.

The yearly Ascension Day 'Dressing of the Wells' is Tissington's way of giving thanks to God for the gift of water. Every year streams of visitors come to admire the unique artistry of the village's many dedicated workers.

'Well-Dressing' has been a custom in the village for almost 600 years. It started in the fourteenth century, when the purity of Tissington's water, flowing cold and clear from its limestone springs, is believed to have saved the village from the terrible 'Black Death' plague which struck so many neighbouring Derbyshire towns.

As Jenny and her father reached the village square, dozens of Tissington's 'well-dressers' were already busily at work. Huge twenty-foot frames, one for each of the five wells, had been covered with a thin coating of soft clay on which five different scenes from the Bible were outlined. Now, thousands of brightly coloured flower petals were being pressed into the clay and the biblical pictures were taking vivid shape. Baskets of flowers, leaves and moss, which Jenny had helped to pick and gather, had been placed nearby the workers. Jenny joined the other children in plucking the petals from the flowers and handing them to her father and the other dressers who were busily at work on the picture frames.

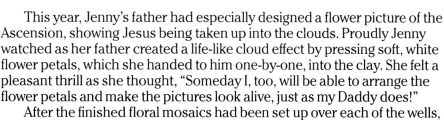

This year, Jenny's father had especially designed a flower picture of the Ascension, showing Jesus being taken up into the clouds. Proudly Jenny watched as her father created a life-like cloud effect by pressing soft, white flower petals, which she handed to him one-by-one, into the clay. She felt a pleasant thrill as she thought, "Someday I, too, will be able to arrange the flower petals and make the pictures look alive, just as my Daddy does!"

After the finished floral mosaics had been set up over each of the wells, Jenny and her father joined Jenny's mother for the Ascension Day service at their village church. Jenny could hardly contain her excitement as, after the service, the entire village and its many hundreds of visitors formed a procession to visit Tissington's five wells; each one now resplendent in flower petal glory. Never before had the floral pictures seemed so beautiful to Jenny and as she heard people praise them, she felt a warm glow, for this year she, too, had taken part in carrying on the ancient tradition of well-dressing at Tissington.

Whitsuntide

Following Ascensiontide comes the Festival of Whitsun. This Festival, also known as Pentecost, celebrates the descent of the Holy Spirit upon the followers of Jesus.

Whitsun takes place in the heart of springtime when nature is at her loveliest. As buds and blossoms open under the influence of the sun, we are given a wonderful picture of how the souls of the disciples opened under the influence of the Holy Spirit at Pentecost.

The Light of the Sun

The light of the sun is flooding
The breadths of space,
The song of the birds is sounding
Through realms of air,

The wakening plants are springing
From depths of earth,
And thankfully the souls of men are rising
To the Spirit of the world.

Rudolf Steiner

With the week of Whitsuntide, we begin the second half of the Christian Calendar Year. During the first half of the year (Advent to Whitsun) our attention has been directed to *what God has revealed to Man,* particularly through the history of Christ becoming Man and of His divine deeds on earth. Now, in the second half of the year (Whitsuntide, Advent) our attention is focused on *Man's response to God* — through faith, through committment, through loving deeds and through trying to understand Christ's transforming work upon the earth and within each individual man and woman. Following the Festivals of this second half of the year gives us the magnificent opportunity of creatively 'responding to God' by searching for new ways to bring true, unselfish love and understanding into the present and future history of our world.

Pentecost

'Pentecost' is the Greek name for the Jewish Harvest Festival of 'Shavuoth' (Sha-voo-oth). 'Pentecost' means 'fifty', for this feast of thanksgiving takes place fifty days after the Jewish Passover. The day of Pentecost is also exactly fifty days after the Resurrection of Jesus.

Whitsun

The English name for the Festival of Pentecost is 'Whitsun' or 'White Sunday' because of the white garments worn by the many people baptised on that day. Although baptismal services usually took place on the day before Easter, in colder climates baptisms were delayed until the weather was milder — fifty days after Easter — at Pentecost.

Apostles and Disciples

The word 'disciple' means 'learner'. All those who followed the teachings of Jesus were considered His disciples.

The word 'Apostle' means 'one who is sent'. Twelve of Jesus' disciples were sent by Him into the world to preach His Gospel. They became the twelve Apostles: Peter, John, Matthew, Thomas, James, Bartholomew, James son of Alphaeus, Philip, Andrew, Simon, Thaddeus, and Matthias who was chosen, shortly before Pentecost, as the twelfth Apostle. He replaced Judas Iscariot, who had betrayed Jesus.

The Earliest Christian Church

A Pentecost Story

Slowly, Mary climbed the staircase to the upper room of the house in Jerusalem where the disciples of Jesus had gathered to pray. "Today is the tenth day since Jesus disappeared from our view into the world of the clouds," thought Mary. "Oh my Son, my Lord! Send the Holy Spirit, the Comforter, soon. We miss you so!"

It was the Jewish Festival of Shavuoth, also known as Pentecost. As Mary entered the large room, the twelve Apostles and other disciples of Jesus rose to greet her. John and Peter, the two Apostles who were closest to Jesus in love and understanding, led her to a seat in their midst. Mary saw the look of grief and discouragement on many of their faces. She understood how alone and empty they felt.

"Children, children, brothers and sisters," Mary said softly, "we all miss Him. For nine days and nights we have prayed together, without seeing Him or hearing Him speak. But this is the day when our people give thanks to God for the fruits of the harvest and for the blessing of the Ten Commandments which God gave Moses on Mount Sinai. We, who love Jesus, have even more to be thankful for. And He has promised that He will send us the Holy Spirit!

Let us pray together, thankfully, joyfully, with open hearts, ready to receive *whatever* He wishes us to experience."

For a long time the followers of Jesus prayed together. Suddenly, there came a sound like the rushing of a mighty wind. The disciples beheld flames, like cloven tongues of fire, which descended from heaven upon each one of them. They became filled with the Holy Spirit! Enlightenment flashed up within each of them. All at once they truly understood the magnificence of the life, the death and the Resurrection of Jesus Christ and what He had taught them. They now received a new power, the healing power of the Holy Spirit, working from within each one of them.

Joyfully they embraced one another. No longer were they afraid. Filled with strength and courage they went forth to tell everyone about Jesus Christ.

People from many lands had come to Jerusalem for the Festival of Pentecost. The Apostles began to speak in a new language, like a language of love, given them by the Holy Spirit. As an amazing miracle, every man, from every country, heard and understood what the Apostles were saying, each in his own language. The news of this miracle spread throughout Jerusalem. Crowds flocked to see and hear the Apostles. Peter preached a great sermon, and three thousand people became followers of Jesus Christ.

And so, on that Pentecost day, the baptism of the Holy Spirit, which Jesus had promised, came to each of the disciples. It gave them peace and joy and the power of love, which allowed them to share everything they had with others. It changed them from a disorganised and frightened group into inspired and fearless leaders of a movement which changed the world. With the descent of the Holy Spirit, the earliest Christian church was born.

John the Baptist

According to the Gospels of Matthew, Luke and John

Fear not, Zacharias . . . thy wife Elisabeth shall bear thee a son, and thou shalt call his name John . . . and many shall rejoice at his birth.

The Archangel Gabriel — Luke 1:13,14b

And thou, child, shalt be called the prophet of the Highest: for thou shalt go before the face of the Lord to prepare his ways.

Zacharias — Luke 1:76

And the child grew, and waxed strong in spirit, and was in the deserts till the day of his showing unto Israel.

Luke 1:80

. . . the word of God came unto John the son of Zacharias in the wilderness. And he came into all the country about Jordan, preaching the baptism of repentance for the remission of sins.

Luke 3:2,3

I *am* the voice of one crying in the wilderness, Make straight the way of the Lord . . .

Behold the Lamb of God, which taketh away the sin of the world.

. . . this my joy therefore is fulfilled. He must increase, but I *must* decrease.

John the Baptist — John 1:23,29b and 3:29,30

And he [Herod] sent, and beheaded John in the prison.

Matthew 14:10

And Jesus said:

Verily I say unto you, Among them that are born of women there hath not risen a greater than John the Baptist.

. . . he bare witness unto the truth.

He was a burning and shining light.

Matthew 11:11a and John 5:33, 35a

'Tis Ur-i-el, Archangel stern,
Whose warning glance bids us to turn
Our gaze beyond both joy and care,
To search for Spirit everywhere;
Then as our hearts rise high above,
God touches us with His own Love.

The Festival of John the Baptist

June 24 — A Midsummer Festival of Man

Every year on this day, the image of John the Baptist heralds the coming of summer. The Festivals of this second half of the Christian Year focus attention on *Man responding* to all he has received from God. In many countries this Midsummer* birthday of John is celebrated as a major Festival. Often called the 'Summer Christmas', St. John's Day celebrations are gay and colourful. Garlands of flowers and boughs of green decorate churches and homes. Outdoor gatherings ring with the sound of music, for singing and dancing are a joyful part of the day.

The Festival of John the Baptist is very old. It was celebrated by the earliest Christians. As the message of Christianity spread throughout the Roman Empire, the Church brought the powerful image of John the Baptist before its new followers at the time of Midsummer for a special reason.

John had been born at the summer solstice**, the longest day of the year when the sun has reached its highest point in the heavens. On this day many pre-Christian peoples, including the Romans, the Celts and the northern Germanic tribes, held Nature Festivals to honour the power of the sun and to 'receive the light'. On the eve of the solstice great bonfires were lighted, which burned until dawn to welcome the sun on the day of is highest powers. These ancient peoples became filled with an ecstasy, but as they danced and leaped among the sparks which rose high into the sky from their fires, they often worked themselves into a wild frenzy. A kind of 'Midsummer madness' took possession of them.

The Church brought to the Midsummer Festivals the message which John the Baptist had preached: "Change! Repent! Let go of the old ways and receive the New Light of the Spirit which Christ brings." The Church declared that the bonfires would henceforth honour John the Baptist, whom Jesus had called, "A burning and a shining light." The bonfires became a symbol for purification; for 'burning away' old faults and ideas which were no longer desired.

Today, in our time, celebrating the Festival of John the Baptist can bring a wonderful sense of harmony and balance. In the cycle of the year, the nativity of John is exactly opposite to Christmas. In the winter when the world appears to be barren and cold, we celebrate the birth of Jesus. In the warmth and lushness of summer at the time of John's birth, we celebrate Christ's working in the world, within nature since the Resurrection and Ascension, and within mankind since the Descent of the Holy Spirit.

St. John's Day is a Christian Festival of Nature. It calls on us to look at nature with 'new eyes'; enjoying it to the fullest, yet always aware that behind its beauty God is at work.

John the Baptist's Day is a Festival of Man as well, for it calls upon us to think about the very best that is within us. The old Midsummer message 'receive the light' is now changed and becomes 'receive Christ's Light! Become what you truly are — MAN — made in the image and likeness of God.'

Although the day is commonly called 'Midsummer', summer is only just beginning.

**During earlier times the summer solstice fell on June 24 but as a result of astronomical and calendar changes, June 24 now falls about three days after the solstice. The word 'solstice' means 'sun-stands-still'.*

A Burning and a Shining Light

The Prophet John the Baptist

By the sun-scorched, uninhabited banks of the River Jordan a crowd of people stand and listen, spellbound; hardly daring to breathe, as the voice of the prophet John thunders forth in mighty words the message which through him comes from God. Not for four hundred years has God sent a prophet to the people of Israel. Not for four hundred years have the people of Israel heard a man preach that which the Spirit speaks through him; and not just in words he has learned from studying the scriptures.

In his dress and appearance John is also like the Prophets of old. His hair and beard are long and his rough garment is woven from camel hair. Tied around his waist is a crude leather belt. John's eyes blaze with the fire of the Spirit and his God-given words have power which stirs the very souls of his listeners. "I am the voice of one crying in the wilderness," he tells the assembled crowd. "Repent! The long-awaited Messiah is about to appear! Repent — change your minds and hearts so that you will be able to receive Him and be saved!"

Abruptly John's mood changes. He becomes quieter. His voice grows softer and the blazing fire in his eyes is replaced by an almost gentle glow. He allows questions to come from the crowd and replies with practical advice to each questioner. He tells them that man must now live from an individual sense of right and wrong, not only by the laws given by Moses.

At last one man asks the question that many are thinking, "We know that God is speaking through you. Are *you* then the Messiah whom we, the people of Israel, long for?"

"I am not worthy even to tie the sandal straps of the One who will come," John declares. "I baptise with water, but He shall baptise with the Holy Spirit and with fire."

Once again the fervour and fire of John's words increases and he cries out, "Oh Israel! Make yourselves ready for Him. Confess your sins — your mistakes — give up your old ways! Come and be baptised!"

Deeply moved by his words, people crowd to the river's edge. One by one they step into the water and are baptised by John and his disciples.

Many who are baptised have wonderful experiences and visions. Old limitations and fears are 'washed away'. They feel purified and see the world as if through new eyes. They become ready to receive the new saving grace that the promised Messiah will bring.

On a certain day, after months of preaching and baptising, John, as he stands in the River Jordan, looks up and sees a young man approaching him. It is Jesus. John gasps as a sudden flash of illumination strikes him. Then softly he exclaims, "The Lamb of God!"

And when Jesus stands before John and asks to be baptised, John humbly answers, "It is I who have need to be baptised by you!"

The two men look into each other's eyes. Then Jesus tells him, "Let it be as I have said. Both of us should do what is right in the eyes of God."

John performs the baptism, there in the waters of the River Jordan. And as Jesus rises from the water and begins to pray, John beholds the heavens open. The Holy Spirit, in the shape of a dove, descends upon Jesus Christ and remains with Him. John hears a voice from heaven saying, "This is my beloved Son."

The Mission

One may wonder what were the thoughts and images and feelings that surged through the soul of John the Baptist after the glorious and over-powering experience of recognising and baptising Christ, the Son of God. After the baptism John announced to his disciples that Jesus was the Messiah he had told them to expect. Now that John's life-time mission on earth had been completed, he must have looked back over the thirty years of his life. He must have recalled his many years in the desert wilderness while he was preparing himself — fasting, studying, praying, meditating, making himself ready for the moment when Spirit began to speak through him.

From his earliest years John had known that he was destined to announce the coming of the Messiah. Even the circumstances surrounding John's birth revealed that. John was an only child. His father, Zacharias, a priest of the Temple in Jerusalem, was quite old when John was born; and his mother, Elisabeth, was well beyond the age of child-bearing. For many years Zacharias and Elisabeth had prayed in vain for God to send them a child. Then, when they had lost all hope, the Archangel Gabriel had appeared to Zacharias as he was serving in the Temple. "Your wife, Elisabeth, shall bear you a son," the Angel had told him. "You shall call his name John and he will be great in the sight of the Lord." Through his meeting with the Angel, Zacharias had lost the power of speech. Not until after his son had been born and named John, as the Angel had directed, was Zacharias able to speak again. Then for a few moments, the Spirit had spoken through Zacharias proclaiming that John would be called the Prophet of the Highest, and prepare the way for the Messiah.

John may have pondered, too, other mysterious ways in which God works. He knew that Jesus was his own cousin — for Mary, the mother of Jesus, was the cousin of John's mother, Elisabeth. Both women had spent three months together while they were waiting for their sons to be born. Yet God had not revealed to John that Jesus was to be the Messiah until that overwhelming moment of revelation at the River Jordan.

After the baptism several of John's followers, including Andrew and Peter, became the first disciples of Jesus. John had prepared them well. For a few months longer, John continued to baptise and preach, always pointing the way to the Messiah. During this time, John's popularity rose to new heights. Yet, with wisdom and understanding, when speaking of Christ John told his own disciples, "He must increase, but I must decrease."

Fearless as ever, John denounced wrong-doing wherever he found it! When he spoke out against the corruption of Herod Antipas, the ruler of Galilee, John was arrested. After many months in prison he was beheaded at the order of Herod.

After his death, the disciples of Jesus felt John's spiritual presence among them, inspiring them to carry out their great earthly work.

Midsummer Night and Midsummer Day Celebrations

Night-time stars and bonfires bright,
Families and friends sing on good St. John's Night.
Summer sun, the sweet smell of hay,
And children all dancing on Midsummer Day.

In Scandinavia, Spain and most Spanish-speaking countries, Greece, France and the Canadian Province of Quebec, the Birthday of John the Baptist is celebrated as a major Festival of the year. Until recently, on the eve of this Day, flaming bonfires lighted the countryside all over Great Britain and Europe. In parts of Italy, it is celebrated with solemn processions.

Bonfire celebrations are traditional on the eve of the Festival of John the Baptist*, and dining under the stars, singing and folk dancing are a joyous part of the festivities. Each region has is own traditional type of winding dance in which the dancers circle clockwise around the fire imitating the path of the sun as it rises in the east and sets in the west. As the bonfires die down, young and old take turns in jumping over the coals to symbolise 'burning away' their troubles, faults, bad tempers and grumbles!

In Scandinavian countries, bonfires are frequently built on mountain-heights where they can be seen for miles. Young people dressed in native costumes and singing old folk songs row out onto the fjords and lakes to watch the beauty of the burning fires reflected many times in the clear water.

In Spain, especially in Catalonia and in the Pyrenees, celebrations are most elaborate. Special pastries called 'cocas', made with pine-nuts and sweet fruits, are eaten with relish.

In some Spanish villages children spend days collecting wood and old furniture to pile up in village squares, ready to be lit as a great bonfire on St. John's Eve. In other villages, youngsters climb the mountains to find large pine branches to be used as torches. At midnight they set fire to the branches and carry them down to the square outside the village church. There, the flaming torches are joined to make an enormous bonfire.

On the island of Puerto Rico, thousands of people throng to the beaches on the Eve of the *Fiesta de San Juan Bautista*. Soon bonfires appear everywhere on the sands and the sound of singing and guitar music fill the night air. At midnight, re-enacting the old custom of 'washing away one's sins', everyone plunges into the ocean — many still wearing their street clothes! Picnics and barbecues and laughter and music follow. Then, weary but happy, everyone goes home to await the morning ringing of church bells, calling them to special services.

For city dwellers, open fires are not practical, so in place of a bonfire, a circle of candles is a lovely alternative. Two dozen candles, placed in glass candle holders or jars on the ground and arranged in a ring, provide a 'fiery' centre for an evening celebration with family and friends.

In the Canadian Province of Quebec, St. John's Day is celebrated as a national holiday. In the capital city of Montreal, there is a spectacular parade. The central float carries a little boy dressed as a shepherd, representing John as a child, and beside him is a white, fleecy lamb.

On Midsummer Day, dancing around a 'St. John's tree' is a favourite custom in many countries. Each country has its own variety of 'tree'. Some are simple poles or crosses adorned with greens and flowers, some are pyramids, decked with garlands and blossoms.

*June 23 is also referred to as both St. John's Night and St. John's Eve.

Midsummer Fairy Folklore

For centuries, folklore has held that on Midsummer's Eve all the fairy-folk gather for the Festival of Fairies. Even today, some children leave out tiny bits of fruits or sweets for the fairies on Midsummer Eve, just as on Christmas Eve they leave cake and hot cocoa for Santa Claus, or Father Christmas.

At Midsummer time the fairies come out,
If children could see them with glee they would shout!
On Midsummer's Eve even gnomes try to dance,
In fairy-ring revels they awkwardly prance.
On Midsummer Day elves and fairies all fly
From acorns and buttercups up to the sky.

The Wisest Son
A Fable of Light and Wisdom

A wise old king called his three sons to him. "Before I die, I wish to learn which of you is the wisest," he said. "I will give to each of you a small silver coin. Buy something that will fill my room."

The oldest went at once to buy straw. The second bought feathers. The youngest son thought and thought. At last he found his answer and made a purchase.

That evening the oldest son spread his straw in his father's room but it covered only the floor of the room. The second son scattered his feathers but they filled only half the room.

Quietly, the youngest son took out a candle and lit it with a match. The whole room filled, from floor to ceiling, with a warm glow.

The old king smiled and said, "Though you are my youngest son, you are the wisest. You shall rule the land after me for I know you will manage it well and bring light to my people."

The Fire of Love

Some day, after mastering the winds,
the waves, the tides, and gravity,
we shall harness for God the energies
of Love, and then, for the second time
in the history of the world, man
will have discovered fire.

P. Teilhard de Chardin

A Canticle for Brother Sun

Praised be You, My Lord, in all Your creatures,
Especially Sir Brother Sun,
Who makes the day and enlightens us through You.
He is lovely and radiant and grand;
And he heralds You, his Most High Lord.

St. Francis of Assisi

The Story of Michael and the Dragon

According to the Book of Revelation

And there was war in heaven: Michael and his angels fought against the dragon; and the dragon fought and his angels, And prevailed not; neither was their place found any more in heaven.

And the great dragon was cast out, that old serpent, called the Devil, and Satan, which deceiveth the whole world: he was cast out into the earth, and his angels were cast out with him.

Revelation 12:7-9

Great Mi-cha-el, Archangel Strong,
Helps us to conquer all that's wrong!
When in our minds we see his face,
Which touched by Christ sheds radiant grace,
We gain new strength by day and night
To bring to darkness healing light.

Michaelmas

September 29 — The Festival of Courage

Autumn has arrived! The first frosts have come, turning the leaves on the trees to gold and crimson. The summer fruits have ripened and farmers are gathering in the harvest. Nuts and acorns and seeds of every kind fall to earth and await the transformation that a new season will bring. Nature's robust life, so evident in the spring and summer, is fading away.

For people, too, the rhythm is changing. School has begun for children. Men and women are taking on new projects. It is time to 'come into ourselves', to wake up out of the summer-holiday-dreaminess in which it was so easy to be 'out there' with the blue sky and the clouds.

The dramatic picture of the Archangel Michael, with his shining spirit-sword of iron and light, was the image used by Christians long ago to remind them to 'wake up' at this turning point of the Year.

Since the sixth century, the Festival of the Archangel Michael and All Angels has been celebrated on September 29, soon after the autumn equinox. It was once one of the most important Festivals of the year, for the image of Michael conquering the dragon was a real part of every Christian's daily life. This image gave them courage and hope in their fight against the 'dragons' that hide within each person's inner nature. Not only did people love and feel reverence for Michael as a true messenger of God, they looked up to him for guidance and help. Even today, the picture of Michael conquering the dragon is a powerful one which brings courage and hope, even to the faint-hearted.

Michaelmas falls during the second half of the Christian Year; the time which can be regarded as 'Man's creative response to what God is giving and revealing'. A modern celebration of Michaelmas can be part of that response. It is also a statement of Man's appreciation for the help of our constant, invisible companions, the Angels, and for their leader, the Archangel Michael.

"Every visible thing in this world is put under the charge of an Angel."

St. Augustine of Hippo

Fair Customs of Michaelmas

Now the Harvest is in,
There is grain in the bin,
Through hard work and God's aid
The year's rent has been paid.

The Sheriff's elected,
Each Judge is selected,
The geese are all fat —
There is milk for the cat,

And with pennies to spare
We are off to a Michaelmas Fair!

Festive costumes, food stalls, music and dancing, games and livestock shows, winning prizes — all of these are part of the excitement of going to a Harvest Fair during Michaelmas season. In England there are still even special 'Goose Fairs'. Eating goose on Michaelmas was a favourite English custom and was believed to bring good luck. Most tenant farmers had to present their landlords with at least one fat 'Michaelmas Goose' along with their yearly land-rent which also became due at Michaelmas.

Michaelmas also became the day for selecting public officials, for the Archangel Michael is known as the protector of men. In England the custom arose of appointing or electing sheriffs, magistrates and other protectors of the people on Michaelmas Day. England's fair customs of Michaelmas will long be remembered!

Michael Legends

In the torch-lit halls of castles and around village fires, bards and minstrels sang of the valiant deeds of Michael, the Archangel. Many of these legends originated with the Church Fathers themselves and told of those times when Michael had appeared to men on earth. Others were local legends which sprang from the hearts of the simple people as 'word-pictures' of how they venerated Michael!

The Devil's Challenge

Once, the crafty, scheming Devil, trying to get the better of Michael, taunted the Archangel and said, "My power on earth has no limits!"

"God alone is all-powerful" replied Michael.

"Well then," challenged the Devil, "call on God to build a castle and I will build one, too. Then we shall see which castle is the more splendid!"

When the Archangel Michael agreed, the Devil sent out a legion of lesser devils to bring huge granite blocks from all over the world and drop them on a small island surrounded by fierce waves. Through their hard labour, a tall mountain arose, on top of which was built a great stone castle. "Match that if you can!" cried the Devil.

The Archangel Michael held up his sword of light. At once, an exquisite castle of ice-crystals sprang up. Its transparent walls, dauntless towers and delicate columns shimmered and sparkled like diamonds. Even the proud Devil had to admit that it was far more splendid than the sombre granite castle. Filled with envy, he could not rest until, at last, he persuaded the Archangel Michael to exchange castles with him.

How pleased the Devil was to live within such sparkling splendour! But when the summer came, the Devil found himself homeless. His castle of ice-crystals had melted under the sun — while the granite castle of the Archangel Michael, re-dedicated to God, is still standing. And through the centuries it has been known as 'Mont St. Michel'.

A Peasant Legend from Normandy

The Miracle of Monte Sant' Angelo

In the small city of Sipontus, in Southern Italy, there lived in the fourth century a wealthy man named Garganus. This rich man and his servants once searched all day for a young bull that had strayed. At last they found the bull standing at the mouth of a cave atop a steep mountain near their city. Garganus, angry with the animal for causing him so much trouble, drew his bow and shot an arrow at the bull. The arrow suddenly turned around and struck Garganus. In amazement the people of the city went to their bishop to ask why this strange thing had happened.

"Fast and pray to God for an answer," said the bishop. After three days the Archangel Michael appeared, and said, "The cave is my special place on earth. It is to be kept holy. I could not allow Garganus to profane it."

The bishop then led a great procession up to the mountain top, where everyone knelt in prayer. From that time the mountain has been called Monte Sant' Angelo*, and known as a 'Holy Place of Michael'.

Retold from 'The Golden Legend' by Voragine

*Church legends tell that the Archangel himself appeared to give instructions for the founding of his three great mountain churches — Mont St. Michel in France, Monte Sant' Angelo (also called Mount Gargano) in Italy, and St. Michael's Mount in England.

Michael Conquers the Dragon

God created heaven and the Heavenly Host. There were thousands of Angels and many Princely Angels, called Archangels*, among them Gabriel, Raphael, Uriel and their leader, Michael, whose name means 'Who is like unto the Lord'. Seven shining Archangels stood before the Throne of God the Father and with them stood a brilliant, high and powerful being called 'Lucifer'**.

All the Heavenly Host enjoyed God's glory in harmony, until one day Lucifer declared, "I am beautiful and powerful! I can change myself into all kinds of shapes and forms. Why should I not have my throne above all the stars and be as important as God?" Lucifer persuaded many other Angels to follow him in their rebellion against God's rule.

The Archangel Michael, ever faithful to God, gathered an army of loyal Angels and they battled against Lucifer's army — which appeared in the heaven as a great and fiery dragon called the Devil, or Satan. It was a fierce battle until at last Michael, with his gleaming sword, drove Lucifer out of heaven and into the earth. Then the gates of heaven were closed against Lucifer.

On earth, the power of the dragon causes evil by sending deceitful thoughts, like dragon-dust, to cloud the minds and hearts of men. The dragon hopes to keep mankind from reaching the heaven from which he was banished. But Michael stands, ever ready, to protect each man and woman and child when they earnestly ask his help.

*'Arch' means 'prince'; 'Angel' means 'messenger'.
**The name 'Lucifer' means 'bearer of light'.

The Crowd Within

Within my earthly temple there's a crowd,
There's one of us who's humble, one who's proud;
There's one who's broken-hearted for his sins,
And one who, unrepentent, sits and grins.
There's one who loves his neighbour as himself,
And one who cares for naught but fame and self.
From this confusing crowd would I be free —
If once I could discover which is me?

Oh, No!

For in my inner kingdom I can find
An opposite for every 'self' that's kind!
I have a brave one, coward, wise one, fool
A loving child and oh, a stubborn mule!
From childhood to death they've much to say —
In fact they speak up loudly every day;
There's many I would cheerfully disown
But there's no doubt they call my temple 'home' —
And facing that they're here is far more wise,
For then they cannot take me by surprise.
I want to hear what each 'self' has to say
So I can choose which promptings to obey!
Yes — as I calmly face each different 'me'
Then I begin to learn how to be free.

111

St. George

"Wherever the power of the dragon holds sway on earth, let me go to battle to overcome it in the name of Jesus Christ!" prayed St. George. This famous Patron Saint of England, whose name, George, means 'earth worker', is the Archangel Michael's representative on earth. Although his own special day in the Christian calendar is April 23, his story also belongs to the celebration of Michaelmas.

George was born during the third century in Cappadocia, a mid-eastern part of the Roman Empire, where his father was governor. Even while still a very young man he became one of the few Christian officers in the Roman army. He fought bravely in many battles and became the symbol of Christian Knighthood. For more than a thousand years St. George has been the most revered saint and martyr throughout the Christian world.

In Britain, until modern times, the battle cry, "For England and St. George," inspired British soldiers to feats of bravery. He has been a popular hero, with stories of his deeds filling the imagination of children in much the same way as the exploits of Superman and Luke Skywalker (of *Star Wars*) fill the imaginations of modern children.

The most famous legend about St. George is the story of how he conquered the dragon. In some versions of this legend, St. George slays the dragon. In other versions he conquers the dragon but allows it to live and serve mankind after its power has been transformed.

St. George and the Dragon

The people of Silene, in a far-off Roman province, lived in constant terror! Every day a ferocious dragon rose out of the depths of a nearby lake and prowled around the walls of their city. It roared and struck the walls with its great tail and its hot breath poisoned the air and drove off the armed men who were sent to fight against it.

To keep this terrible dragon from destroying their city, the people had to feed the dragon two sheep every day. Finally there came a time when there were no more sheep and the city was forced to sacrifice its young men and women to the dragon.

One day young St. George, carrying his white shield with a red cross upon it, came riding toward the city. On his way he passed by the shore of the lake where he found an innocent young maiden weeping pitifully. She was the king's daughter and it was now her turn to be sacrificed to the dragon. Quickly St. George dismounted and offered to help her.

"Ride away at once!" the maiden warned him. "Any moment the dragon will come to get me. If you remain here it will devour you as well!"

St. George refused to leave and after the princess told him the whole story he said, "Don't be afraid, for in the name of Christ I will save you."

Just then, rearing its head out of the lake, the dragon, with a terrible roar, approached the maiden. Quickly St. George mounted his horse, took up his sword and his lance, and rushed upon the ferocious dragon. They fought fiercely until at last St. George struck a blow that stunned the dragon and knocked it to the ground. St. George then called upon the pure and innocent young virgin to take from around her waist her girdle, woven from gold and silver threads, and to place it around the dragon's neck.

The Legend Continues . . .

Two accepted endings of 'St. George and the Dragon' are included. Both have been part of this famous Legend throughout the centuries.

As the Dragon is Slain

The pure and innocent maiden obeyed and, as the silver and gold threads of her girdle encircled the dragon's neck, the beast's evil power was overcome. Like a dog on a leash, the dragon then quietly followed the maiden and St. George toward the city.

The people of Silene, who were not Christians, saw the dragon entering their city and were terrified. They ran away to hide. St. George called out to them, "Do not fear but believe in Jesus Christ and, through His power, I shall slay the beast that persecuted you." The king of Silene and his people returned and were baptised. And on that day St. George, keeping his promise, slew the dragon.

For a time, St. George remained in the city, teaching the people about Christianity, and a great church was built to honour him.

Retold from 'The Golden Legend' by Voragine

As the Dragon is Transformed

The fiery dragon, with bloodshot eyes, looked venomously at the innocent maiden as she drew near, carrying her girdle of gold and silver threads. Only St. George's lance, held at the throat of the dragon, kept it from harming the maiden. But in the moment that she cast her girdle around the dragon's neck, a piercing cry came forth from the creature, and before the eyes of St. George and the maiden, the dragon became transformed into a pure white lamb!

St. George then called out to the people to believe in the power of Jesus Christ.

All the people of Silene rejoiced and those who were not Christians began to believe in Jesus Christ and asked to be baptised. The transformed white lamb lived in their midst, always at the side of the princess; and there followed many miracles of healing.

From the legends of the Eastern Church

Angels! Angels Everywhere!

"Mother, how can I get to know the Angels?" ten-year-old Cynthia asked eagerly, as she sat down at the kitchen table and helped herself to a jam-covered muffin.

Mrs. Crawford joined Cynthia at the table and, with a quizzical smile, asked, "What brings on this sudden question? You've only just come home from a football match with your father."

"That's just it," replied Cynthia, "you've always told me that my Guardian Angel is with me wherever I am. When Daddy said that there were thousands of people at the game, I suddenly thought that there must also be thousands of Angels there too, right in the stadium! With so many Angels around I think we should all get to know them better. Yet many of my friends — even at church — don't really believe there are Angels all around us. Why?"

Mrs. Crawford smiled as she answered gently, "I don't know, dear. Perhaps it's difficult for them to accept the idea that we have ever-present invisible companions even though the Bible tells us so in nearly three hundred places. It tells us that God has countless Angels at His command who constantly guide and protect us. And modern Christian leaders, as well as the founders of most Christian denominations, have spoken of their belief in the Lord's Angel Messengers."*

"Mother, what do you suppose Angels really look like?"

"Well, Angels are spirit and spirit is invisible to our eyes; but the Bible tells us that Angels can 'put on' different forms. At times they can appear in bodies that look like human bodies. At other times they appear in bodies which are made up of light and not solid like our bodies."

"How can I get to know more about Angels, Mother?"

"Spend time thinking about them, Cynthia, and feeling their presence with you wherever you are."

Mrs. Crawford thought that Cynthia might soon lose interest in getting to know about Angels, but as time passed the little girl's feeling for Angels grew stronger. Mrs. Crawford's interest in Angels also grew as they began to read earlier Christian teachings concerning Angels.

They learned that the word 'Angels' is used to describe the whole Heavenly Host, which is often said to be made up of nine different classes or orders of Angelic Beings, which form three Hierarchies. Each member of the Hierarchy has different qualities and tasks. The first and most powerful is composed of the *Seraphim,* the *Cherubim* and the *Thrones.* The second Hierarchy is formed of the *Dominations, Virtues* and *Powers.* The Third Hierarchy is made up of *Principalities, Archangels* and *Angels.*

Cynthia and her mother also read the many passages in the Bible where Angels are mentioned. Cynthia's favourite story tells of a special day when Jesus was teaching His disciples and called a little child to Him. Then Jesus said, "Take care that you do not despise one of these little ones, for their Angels always behold the face of my Father in Heaven."**

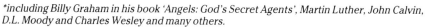

*including Billy Graham in his book 'Angels: God's Secret Agents', Martin Luther, John Calvin, D.L. Moody and Charles Wesley and many others.
**Matthew 18:10

Lucifer's Jewel and the Holy Grail

A Legend

Once, when Lucifer was still a prince of heaven, and before his pride made him rebel against God, he carried in his crown a magnificent, ever-changing jewel! It shimmered like an emerald, blazed like a diamond or took on the glowing red of the ruby or the blue of the sapphire. When the Archangel Michael battled with Lucifer and drove him from the heavens, the wonderful jewel broke from Lucifer's crown and fell to earth. There it became tarnished, and lay as base metal in the earth for thousands of years.

Legends tell that Joseph of Arimathea, a follower and true believer of Christ, was a metalsmith and that it was he who made a cup from that base metal which had been the magnificent jewel in Lucifer's crown. When Jesus drank from that cup at the Last Supper, the cup turned into a silver chalice, glowing like the brightest moon. After the supper Joseph of Arimathea took possession of the chalice, and it was with him as he stood at the foot of the cross on which Jesus was dying. As Joseph caught some of the healing blood from Christ's wounds in the silver chalice, it changed into a golden Grail, which gleamed like the sun. After Christ's death and resurrection, Angels hovered above the Holy Grail. The Grail became ever-changing; now silvery and glowing like the moon, now golden and gleaming like the sun. At times it could be seen with man's physical eyes; at other times it could be seen only with inner spiritual eyes. Throughout all the Grail Legends the sacred chalice appears, then disappears. It was told that it appeared many times to people in the early centuries of Christianity; but only a few, symbolised by Sir Galahad and Parsifal, were able to prepare themselves to gaze on the Grail in the right way so that they could receive the Christ, just as the Grail received His blood.

Legends of the Holy Grail

The English coast was shrouded in mist as Joseph of Arimathea stepped ashore. Forty years had passed since the Crucifixion. Joseph, the follower of Christ who had lovingly taken His body from the cross, had come as a missionary to Britain. Inside Joseph's cloak, held close to his heart, was the Holy Grail, the sacred cup from which Jesus drank at the Last Supper. In this same cup, the original chalice of Communion, Joseph had caught drops of the blood which Jesus shed on the cross. Joseph of Arimathea taught the Christian faith to the people of England and founded an abbey in Glastonbury. There the sacred cup rested until heathen invaders brought continuous warfare to Britain during the fifth century. The Grail then disappeared!

The loss of the Holy Grail was mourned, not only by the people of Britain, but throughout Christian Europe. Many different Grail legends began to appear. Most of them, however, were not written down until later centuries. In the dramatic German legends, the hero who finally succeeds in his Quest for the Holy Grail is Parsifal. Although knighted by King Arthur, his story is somewhat different from the legends which are better known to the French and English speaking nations. Many of these latter legends were collected and written down in the fifteenth century in books about King Arthur and his Knights of the Round Table. In these stories the 'Grail hero' is Sir Galahad. All legends of the Quest for the Holy Grail are filled with adventure and romance but they have a much deeper meaning as well. They tell of man's search for God and for the 'nourishment' which cannot come from the material world but only from Christ — symbolised by the Holy Grail.

The years of war and confusion during the fifth century were dark and terrible. Many of the lords and barons forgot that they were Christians and returned to old barbaric ways. No gentlewoman could travel without armed guards and the poor were abused and treated without mercy. Then came the great British King, Arthur, who, in 484, defeated the heathen invaders at Mount Badon, near Bath.

King Arthur gathered to his famed Round Table , the finest Christian Knights of Britain and Europe. For many years the Knights of the Round Table rode forth to do battle against all forms of tyranny and oppression. It was also the task of each Knight to fight battles within himself and bring under control the selfish passions which live within every human being. Under King Arthur's inspiration, the Knights of the Round Table restored, and brought to a higher stage, a Christian way of life in England and many parts of Europe.

The Quest for the Holy Grail

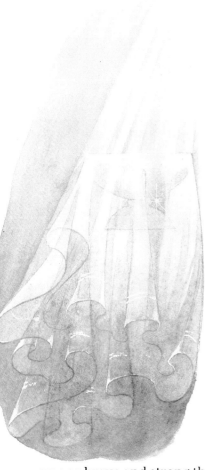

Wherever the Knights of the Round Table might be at other times of the year, it was their custom to gather with King Arthur for the great Christian Feast Days. Each year, at Pentecost, they renewed their vows of Knighthood. One year, as they were seated together on this day, a crash of thunder shook the castle. A shaft of brilliant light entered the hall and seemed to shine right into the hearts of all the Knights. They were filled with awe! As they sat in silence, the Holy Grail appeared in their midst. It was covered by a veil of white samite, a silk cloth interwoven with threads of gold and silver. The Grail floated through the air and circled the table. It hovered for a moment before each of the Knights, leaving each one physically and spiritually refreshed and as satisfied as if he had just eaten of heavenly food. The vision of the Grail then passed from their sight.

Many Knights of the Round Table immediately arose and swore that they would roam the world until they found the Holy Grail. Although warned that only the Knight whose mind was free of guilt over his secret sins could gaze on the sacred chalice without its veil, they went forth in the Quest of the Holy Grail.

Five of the most valiant of the Knights were Sir Lancelot, Sir Percival, Sir Bors, Sir Gawain and Sir Galahad. Each of them encountered many obstacles and perilous adventures. Each was sorely tested. And each would be given another glimpse of the veiled, mystic chalice.

Galahad alone, however, proved himself to be the Knight destined to succeed in the Quest of the Holy Grail. For him, the Quest was the meaning of life. He alone had the courage to make himself ready to receive the full grace of the Grail. When Galahad went to battle for a righteous cause, he was so brave and strong that it was as though the Archangel Michael himself had appeared. And at other times Sir Galahad's sword and shield were used to heal as well as to defend.

After many adventures Sir Galahad found the Holy Grail, and the chalice, still covered with samite, was given into his care to take across the sea to the sacred city of Sarras. There Galahad, with his two faithful companions, Sir Percival and Sir Bors, were imprisoned by the king of Sarras, against the will of the people. After the king's death, the people of Sarras insisted that Sir Galahad become their king for he had brought the Holy Grail to them. Galahad had no wish to be king, and for him the golden crown was as sharp as thorns upon his forehead. Yet with wisdom he reigned over the city for a year.

On a certain Sunday morning, as Sir Galahad knelt to pray before the Holy Grail, the covering of samite was lifted from it. At last Galahad was allowed to look into the uncovered chalice. He trembled with joy and cried out, "Oh, Lord, I give thanks for now I see to the heart of the mystery that passes all understanding. Oh, grant that I may now come to be with you!"

And those who were in the chapel with Sir Galahad, so the legends tell, saw a Hand descend and take up the Holy Grail into heaven. And Angels appeared to escort the soul of Galahad to dwell with the Christ he loved and served so well.

Adapted from the writings of Alfred, Lord Tennyson and Sir Thomas Malory

All Hallows' Tide

Hallowe'en (All Hallows' Eve) October 31
All Saints' Day, November 1
All Souls' Day, November 2

False-face goblins, pirates and fairy princesses, bed-sheet ghosts, grinning Jack-O'-Lanterns, apple bobbing and spooky stories — all of these help make up the most 'be-witching' night of the year, 'Hallowe'en' — celebrated on October 31. What fun it is to wear a costume and a mask, and with them to become a different self or character. There's a kind of shivery excitement about Hallowe'en, yet even the shyest child grows more courageous playing the role of the character whose clothing and 'face' is being worn.

Modern celebrations of Hallowe'en in the English-speaking world have their roots with the Celtic peoples of pre-Christian times. On the last night of October, these ancient peoples began to celebrate a Festival known as 'Samhain'* which means 'Summer's End'. Their priests, called Druids, performed ceremonies to thank and honour the sun. However, this Festival also signalled the approach of winter with its cold bleakness. It was believed that at this time unfriendly ghosts, nature-spirits and witches roamed the earth, creating mischief. The Druid priests lit great bonfires and performed magic rites to ward off or appease these dark supernatural powers.

When the Romans came to Great Britain their customs merged with the customs of Samhain. The Roman Harvest Festival honoured the Goddess Pomona with gifts of apples and nuts.

When Christianity replaced the Roman and Druid religions, November 1 — All Saints' Day — was dedicated to Christian Martyrs and Saints who had died. In Britain this day became known as 'All Hallows' Day'. The evening before became an evening of prayer and preparation and was called 'All Hallows' Eve' (The Holy Evening), later shortened to 'Hallowe'en'. After a time, All Souls' Day, celebrated on November 2, was added to the Church Calendar, reminding everyone to pray for the dead and ask their blessings.

For many centuries, however, fear of the supernatural remained strong. During the Middle Ages, animal costumes and frightening masks were worn to ward off the evil spirits of darkness on Hallowe'en. Magic words and charms were used to keep away bad luck; and the belief in witches riding through the night on broomsticks was commonplace. Fortune telling was widely practised; and predicting the future by the use of nuts and apples became so popular that in parts of Britain, Hallowe'en is still called 'Nutcrack Night' or 'Snap-Apple Night'.

Today, people no longer take these ancient Hallowe'en customs seriously, for through the centuries Christians have learned to turn to prayer instead of 'charms' to overcome the powers of darkness. It is with a sense of fun and adventure that children wear fantasy-costumes and go to Hallowe'en parties where paper witches, black cats and skeletons may decorate the walls.

Grinning Jack-O'-Lanterns carved from pumpkins or large turnips, lit from inside by a candle, can be seen. In the United States and Canada, costumed children ring neighbours' doorbells on Hallowe'en. Their merry threats of 'Trick or Treat' usually bring generous hand-outs of candy, toffee apples and other sweet 'treats'.

The deeper Christian meaning of All Hallows' Eve, however, should not be forgotten. As Christians we all draw closer to Christ when we remember and give thanks for our loved ones and for others who have gone before us through the gates of death.

* Pronounced 'Sah'win'

118

The Land of Memory

A Story for All Hallows' Tide

Ten-year-old Todd and his six-year-old sister Helen were on a journey, searching everywhere for a special Blue Bird which was said to bring happiness. One day their Fairy Godmother told them, "Perhaps you will find a Blue Bird if you visit your grandparents in the Land of Memory."

"But we can't visit them. Our grandparents are dead," exclaimed Todd.

"Oh, no," replied their Fairy Godmother. "They would only be dead if their grandchildren ceased to think of them." Then the fairy took the children to the edge of a forest that was shrouded in mist. She told them to follow the pathway that was carpeted with snow-white pansies.

As the children followed the path they gathered a bouquet of pansies for Grandmother. Each flower (like the 'loving thoughts' which pansies stand for) brought them ever closer and nearer to their grandparents.

All at once the mist disappeared. The children saw ahead a bright and sunny clearing in the midst of the forest. As they drew closer, they suddenly saw their grandparents sitting on a bench in the clearing, fast asleep. Slowly, as the children watched, the old couple awoke. Grandma Tyler stretched and said, "Grandad, I have a notion that our grandchildren are coming to visit us today." And Grandad Tyler answered, "They are certainly thinking of us, for I feel happy and tingly all over."

"We're here! We're here!" cried the children as they ran forward and flung themselves into their grandparents' arms. Oh the kisses and the hugs! How happy all of them were!

"Oh, it's good to see you!" said Grandma Tyler, "it's been so long! Why the last time you were here was at All Hallows' Tide."

The children looked so surprised that Grandma Tyler laughed and said, "Oh, yes, you were here. You were thinking of us. And every time you think of us we see you as clearly as if you were here in person."

Time passed very swiftly for the children while they were in the Land of Memory with their grandparents, for they felt so warm and loved. "We're so glad to know you're really alive here!" exclaimed little Helen.

"Oh, look," cried Todd as a bright little bird flew into the clearing and perched on Grandma's shoulder, "it's a Blue Bird!" And sure enough, just as their Fairy Godmother had told them, the children discovered that Grandad and Grandma did have a Blue Bird of Happiness.

"We'd love to give you our Blue Bird," said Grandma as the children were leaving, "but it belongs to this Land and can only live here with us."

Then Grandad hugged Todd and Helen and said, "Come back soon, children. Don't wait only for All Hallows' Tide. It's such a treat for us whenever your thoughts pay us a visit."

And as Grandma gave the children one last kiss she whispered, "Take this secret with you. Your very own Blue Bird of Happiness is waiting for you, and whenever you look through the eyes of love, you'll find it, right in your own home or wherever you are."

An adaptation based on 'The Blue Bird' by Maurice Maeterlinck

119

Thanksgiving

The Holiday Festival of Thanksgiving will not bé found on traditional Christian Church Calendars. Nor is it celebrated by that name anywhere other than in the United States and Canada, yet perhaps no other holiday so expresses the feeling and spirit with which to complete one cycle of Christian Festivals and begin the new cycle, which starts again with Advent.

For thousands of years, in every land, men, women and children have come together to give thanks at Harvest time. This same spirit of devotion and gratitude was present at the first American Thanksgiving. The story of the Pilgrims, and how they founded this now famous Festival, is inspiring.

The Pilgrims and the First Thanksgiving

The breaking waves had seldom dashed higher on the stern and rock-bound New England coast than they did on December 21, 1620. On that memorable day eighteen men from the ship *Mayflower*, on which they had crossed the Atlantic Ocean from Plymouth, Devon, finally landed their small ship's boat at what is now Plymouth, Massachusetts.

About ten days later, many of the rest of the Pilgrims left the *Mayflower*, and started to build their settlement. At last they had found a land where they could worship God freely, in the way of their own choice.

Their voyage on the *Mayflower* had been long and stormy. The ship was overcrowded and food and supplies were short. Nearly all the passengers were weak and suffering from a variety of ills.

During their first months in America, the Pilgrims endured hardship — hunger, sickness and the bitter cold of the New England winter. When spring came, nearly half of the original one hundred settlers had died. Many others were too weak to begin planting the crops they would need to survive and to live through another winter. The future of the little colony looked bleak indeed. But prayer to the almighty God was a way of life for these men and women.

God's answer to their prayers came in a most unexpected way. One day in mid-March, an Indian brave walked into the Pilgrim settlement and addressed the astonished settlers in their own language. "I am Samoset," he told them. "Welcome!"

Samoset, an Abaki Indian, from what is now the State of Maine, had learned English from traders. He befriended the Pilgrims and soon brought his friend Tisquantum, 'Squanto', to help them as well. Squanto, too, spoke English and he told his amazing story to the settlers.

Several years before, Squanto had been kidnapped by a raiding sea captain and taken to England. There he had been well treated but still longed for his native land. After many adventures Squanto managed to return to America but was again kidnapped and taken on a ship to Spain where he was sold as a slave.

Fortunately, his masters were kindly Christian Friars who taught him their religion. Eventually Squanto escaped and was able to return to New England, only to find that his entire tribe had tragically perished in a great plague.

From the time that Squanto entered the Pilgrims' small settlement, he became their constant companion and adopted their religion. He taught the Pilgrims the many ways of the wilderness which helped them to survive. He taught them how to grow and grind corn; how to dry the sweet summer fruit

and how to hunt and fish. Squanto helped the Pilgrims to negotiate a treaty with the Indian Chief Massasoit, of the Wampanoag Indians, on whose land the Pilgrims had settled. In the words of William Bradford, one of the colony's first Governors, Squanto was, ". . . a special instrument sent of God for their good beyond their expectations."

Autumn in New England is a beautiful season and the Pilgrims' first harvest of Indian corn was plentiful. In gratitude for God's goodness, they decided to hold a Harvest Festival of Thanksgiving and sent Squanto to invite Chief Massasoit to their feast.

On the appointed day in 1621, the little colony — about sixty men, women and children — gathered to receive their guests. Imagine their surprise when Massasoit arrived with about ninety hungry braves, all dressed in animal skins and brightly coloured turkey feathers! How could the Pilgrims possibly feed so many? Massasoit must have noticed the Pilgrims' dismay for at his command, the Indian braves disappeared into the woods. Soon they returned bearing five deer which they helped the Pilgrims roast on spits over open fires.

The day was warm and sunny, and in addition to the deer meat there were wild turkeys and ducks and geese; lobsters, eels, clams and oysters and roast corn. There were cranberries and apple cider and sweet maple syrup to spread upon the corncakes made by the Pilgrim women. It was indeed a Harvest Feast and it continued for three days!

That first Thanksgiving is thought to have been celebrated in October and, to this day, is so celebrated in Canada. The Pilgrims of New England and their descendants celebrated Thanksgiving throughout the years on various dates. In 1863 President Abraham Lincoln proclaimed 'a Day of Thanksgiving' on the fourth Thursday in November. It then became a yearly national holiday in the United States.

This second half of the Christian year (Whitsun to Advent) is thought of as *Man's creative response to God.* Creating the mood and spirit of Thanksgiving is an especially beautiful way to complete the round of the Christian year.

In only a few days, the season of Advent will begin once again. Now is the time to give thanks, *in advance,* that each of us will open our hearts and receive the Christ Child we love, as once again we enter into and follow another of God's Years.

Mala Powers

121

Preparing for Family Celebrations of the Festivals

Be sure to plan ahead for each festival, allowing plenty of time for the special holiday preparations, fun and activities to be shared by parents and children. Heightened devotion and a special family closeness comes about as parents and children develop their own creative home festival celebrations.

Create your own Seasonal Stage

To help children develop a sense of the year's rhythm and a feeling for changes in the seasons, you may wish to participate with them in creating a 'Seasonal Stage' that will dramatise your holidays. The stage could be the corner table or a bookshelf. If you are cramped for space, a movable tray no more than 30cm (12in) in diameter may be used. The display should be changed for each festival or season. As you gather natural greenery and leaves of the season, flowers, stones, crystals, shells — a small pottery dove, angel or elf — you'll have an infinite variety of material.

The Christmas Season

The fourth Sunday before Christmas, the start of Advent, is a good time to begin our most colourful festival with a family prayer, and the lighting of the first candle on an Advent wreath (see page 12). Families gather, beginning on December 1, with children opening one window of an Advent calendar each day until Christmas as mother or father tell or read a Christmas story.

Setting up a Nativity scene is always a treat for children, as are making Christmas decorations for the house, singing Christmas carols and playing Christmas records. Organise your own family Nativity play — or dramatise a short Nativity scene at various times during the season. A particularly nice way to celebrate Three Kings' Day on January 6 is for children to dress up and enact the Wise Men presenting their gifts to the Christ Child.

Candlemas (February 2)

It's time to change and create a new Seasonal Stage. Holly and evergreens make way for available seasonal greenery and flowers (snowdrops, winter aconite, hazel, pussy-willows etc.)

Add several candles. It's fun to decorate them using a small stick dipped into melted wax-crayon stubs. Candlemas Eve can be memorable for children when the family gathers in a darkened room to light candles one by one, until the room is filled with light (see page 58).

Valentine's Day (February 14)

Help children make personalised Valentine greetings for family and friends. Let them know that receiving Valentine messages make others feel 'cared about' (see page 59).

Pancake Day (Shrove Tuesday)

(The day before Lent; the Easter season begins.)

Having a family 'Pancake party' brings attention to the beginning of Lent. Children will enjoy hearing about 'Carnival' and 'Shrove Tuesday' customs which began in olden times (see pages 62-63).

The Easter Season — Lent, Easter, Eastertide

(Lent may begin as early as February 4 or as late as March 10)

Your Seasonal Stage may change two or three times as winter gives way to spring.

Baking with children is fun — serve pretzels for Ash Wednesday (see pages 64-65). Hot cross buns also belong to the Easter season, as do decorated eggs. Making an 'Easter tree' brings special joys to everyone, (see pages 74-76).

For Holy Week

On Palm Sunday place a wooden cross upright in a pot and plant cress seeds around it. The children will observe the cress sprouting during the week. During Holy Saturday night, fresh greenery should be wound around the cross. Hang three coloured eggs on the cross. On Easter Morning the children will awaken to find that the bare cross has now become a beautiful Easter tree of Life.

Ascension Day (forty days after Easter) and Whitsun (ten days later)

The Seasonal Stage should be changed for both of these days, adding as many fresh flowers as possible. For Whitsun decorate with a white dove made from paper or felt.

The Festival of John the Baptist (June 24)

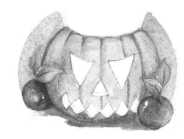

A keynote of this festival and the summer season is the appreciation and enjoyment of nature. Outings to parks, woods or the seashore (to gather shells) are all enriching. An old fashioned (and ever new) St. John's Night celebration (June 23) can be a memorable experience for children — dining under the stars around a bonfire, roasting marshmallows and singing and dancing.

Michaelmas (September 29)

The Seasonal Stage should now include autumn leaves, acorns, nuts, dried grasses or grains; Michaelmas daisies, chrysanthemums or asters — and if possible, an Angel candle-holder or figurine. Learning to preserve leaves and to dry flowers also increases awareness of the Michaelmas season.

Hallowe'en (October 31)

Children love to prepare for Hallowe'en — carving pumpkin or turnip Jack-O'-Lanterns. It is a wonderful time for a party; bobbing for apples and roasting chestnuts. Whether children dress up as ghosts or witches, princes or princesses, wearing Hallowe'en costumes provide each child's 'inner adventurer' with a wonderful opportunity to express a secret desire.

Thanksgiving
October (Canada) — November (USA)

In the United States and Canada, where Thanksgiving is celebrated as a national holiday, cut-out figures of Pilgrims, or a turkey, may be added to the Seasonal Stage, which changes once more. Autumn leaves, nuts, ears of dried corn and harvest fruits make a lovely late autumn display.

As one cycle of the year ends and another is about to begin, modern families everywhere can call up their own mood of thanksgiving as they pray together in gratitude for the love they share — and for all God's blessings.

JANUARY

New Year's Day
(January 1)

Epiphany (Twelfth
Night and Three Kings
Day) (January 6)

Like the Three Kings
we dedicate our
worldy and inner
accomplishments to
Jesus Christ.

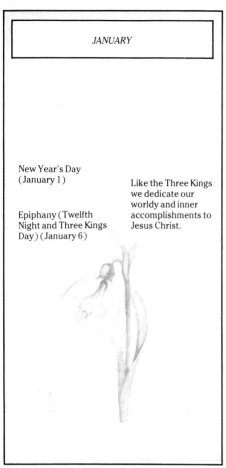

FEBRUARY

Candlemas (February 2)

Valentine's Day
(February 14)
Shrove Tuesday
Ash Wednesday
(Lent Begins) (40 Days
Before Easter)

Light and Love fill our
hearts as we turn our
thoughts to Spring

MARCH

St Patrick's Day
(March 17)
Spring Equinox
(March 20-21)
(The First Day of Spring)
The Annunciation
(March 25)
Palm Sunday

During Lent we seek
to know ourselves
and turn our
weaknesses
to strength.

JULY

In summer we
surrender ourselves to
the beauty of God's
World

AUGUST

The Transfiguration of
Jesus Christ
(traditionally
celebrated on August 6)

We feel in our hearts
the light of God all
around us.

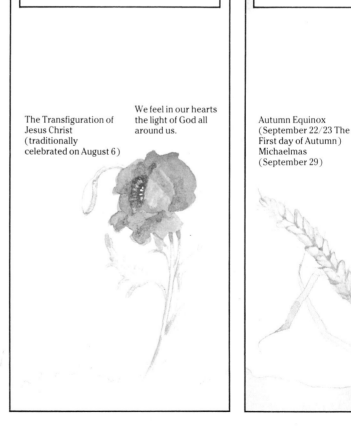

SEPTEMBER

Autumn Equinox
(September 22/23 The
First day of Autumn)
Michaelmas
(September 29)

We seek courage to be
God's helpers on Earth.

APRIL

Holy Week
Maundy Thursday
Good Friday
Easter Sunday
St George's Day
(April 23)

After the sombre mood of Holy Week we rejoice in the Resurrection.

MAY

Mother's Day
Ascension Day
(40 Days After Easter)
Pentecost (Whitsun)
(10 Days after Ascension)
Trinity Sunday

Through Christ we awaken to the power of the Holy Spirit.

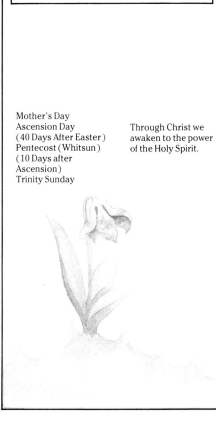

JUNE

Summer Solstice
(June 20-22) (The First Day of Summer)
The Festival
John the Baptist (June 24)
The day of Apostles
Peter and Paul (June 29)

We delight in Nature while remembering we are Man made in God's image.

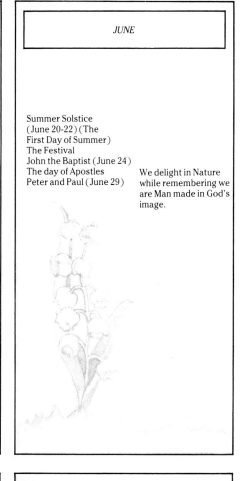

OCTOBER

Thanksgiving in Canada (2nd Monday in October)

As we settle down in Autumn we bring inner strength to our tasks.

Halloween (October 31)

NOVEMBER

All Saints Day
(November 1)
All Souls Day
(November 2)

As we move towards the end of a year we show our gratitude for God's blessings.

Thanksgiving in U.S.A.
(4th Thursday in November)

DECEMBER

Advent
St Nicholas' Day
(December 6)

Santa Lucia Day
(December 13)
Winter Solstice
(December 21/22)
(The first day of Winter)
Christmas Day
(December 25)
Holy Nights begin
(December 25 —
January 6)
New Year's Eve
(December 31)

We prepare for and joyfully celebrate the birth of the Christ Child.

Acknowledgements

The author extends special thanks and appreciation to authors, publishers, and copyright owners for their courteous permissions to adapt and use selections in FOLLOW THE YEAR. Copyright and source acknowledgements are:

Page 11: IT IS NOT FAR, a poem by Ulrich Troubetzkoy in Guideposts Christmas Special, © 1971; used with permission of the publisher. LITTLE CHRIST CHILD, a poem from 'The Christ Candle' by Kate Louise Brown.

Page 12: THE DOUBLE CHRISTMAS GIFT, adapted from 'The Double Gift' by Gerald Horton Bath, reprinted with permission from 'Treasury of Christmas', originally published in Guideposts Magazine, © 1960.

Page 15: THE CHRIST CHILD AND THE BIRDS OF CLAY, adapted from the Apocrypha and from 'In Nazareth' by Selma Lagerlöf.

Page 18: GOD'S CROWNING CREATION, adapted from 'Why God Made Man' in 'How the Stars were Born' by Dan Lindholm, English edition, published by Henry Goulden Ltd. © 1975; used with permission of Verlag Freies Geistesleben.

Page 19: THE SHEPHERD'S FLUTE, adapted from 'The Shepherd's Flute' in 'How the Stars were Born' by Dan Lindholm, English edition published by Henry Goulden Ltd. © 1975; used with permission of Verlag Freies Geistesleben. PICTURE GIFTS, inspired by a true story as told to Mala Powers.

Page 20: ST. FRANCIS AND THE CHRISTMAS CRECHE, adapted from 'Vita Prima' by Thomas Celano, A.D. 1285 approx. HANUKKAH, adapted from The Books of the Maccabees in The Apocrypha.

Page 21: THE 'LUCK BOY' OF TOY VALLEY, by Katherine Dunlap Cather, adapted from 'My Book House', (ed) Olive Beaupré Miller, Copyright 1920, 1923; used with permission of the publisher.

Page 22: A SINGLE CANDLE FLAME, inspired by the poem 'Look to the Light' by Condra Cadle in Daily Word, © 1980 Unity School of Christianity; used with permission of the publisher.

Pages 24-25: A VISIT FROM ST. NICHOLAS by Clement C. Moore originally appeared in the Troy (New York) Sentinel 23 December 1823.

Pages 27-28: WONDER AND JOY, © Mala Powers, an original story based on the Gospel of Luke. SLEEP, HOLY BABE, a poem by Edward Caswell from 'Holy-Days and Holidays' copyright 1902, Funk & Wagnalls Inc.

Pages 29-31: CHRISTMAS IN SUMMER by Charlotte Lohse from 'Merry Christmas to You', (ed) Wilhelmina Harper, copyright 1935, E. P. Dutton & Co., Inc.; used with permission of the Estate of Charlotte Lohse.

Pages 32-34: THE CRIB OF BO'BOSSU from 'The Long Christmas' by Ruth Sawyer, copyright 1941 Ruth Sawyer, renewed © 1968 Ruth Sawyer; adapted by permission of Viking Penguin Inc.

Page 35: A BROTHER LIKE THAT from 'Baskets of Silver', by C. Roy Angell, © 1955, renewed © 1983 Broadman Press; all rights reserved; used by permission.

Pages 36-37: A CHRISTMAS GIFT FOR THE QUEEN, adapted from The Saturday Evening Post, Copyright 1951, used with the permission of The Curtis Publishing Co.

Pages 38-39: THE GIFT OF THE MAGI, adapted from a story in 'The Four Million' by O. Henry, published by Doubleday & Co. Inc.

Pages 40-41: THE YULE LOG AND THE HOLY BABE and WATCH OUT FOR THAT DONKEY, original stories © Mala Powers.

Pages 42-43: FROM ST. NICHOLAS TO FATHER CHRISTMAS AND SANTA CLAUS, adapted from 'From St. Nicholas to Santa Claus' in 'Follow The Star' by Mala Powers, © 1980; used with the permission of Hodder and Stoughton.

Pages 50-51: MIDWINTER NIGHT'S DREAM, an original story © Mala Powers.

Page 54: Four lines from the poem 'In Memoriam' by Alfred, Lord Tennyson.

Pages 56-57: WHAT THE THREE KINGS' BROUGHT, adapted from 'What the Three Kings Brought', a true story in 'Joy to the World' by Ruth Sawyer, © 1966 R. S. Durand; used with permission of Little, Brown & Co.

Page 58: CANDLEMAS, ten lines from the poem 'Ceremonies for Candlemas Eve' by Robert Herrick; THE LOVELIEST OF LIGHTS, a poem by James Dillet Freeman in Daily Word, © 1983 Unity School of Christianity; used with permission of the author. WHEN DAYS ARE DARKEST, a poem by P. S. Moffat in 'The Keys of the Kingdom', published by Rudolf Steiner Press.

Page 63: RUN TO THE CHURCH WITH A FRYING PAN, a poem by Eleanor Farjeon in 'The Children's Bells', published by Oxford University Press.

Page 66: REALITY, a poem by Viola Lukawiecki in Daily Word, © 1976 by Unity School of Christianity; used with permission of the author. A WORD, from an untitled poem in 'The Secret Iron of the Heart' by Arvia MacKaye Ege, © 1982, published by Adonis Press; used with the permission of the author. The last stanza of a poem WHO HAS SEEN THE WIND? by Christina G. Rossetti is used with acknowledgement.

Page 67: THE LADY OF THE BRIGHTLY COLOURED EGGS, adapted from the translation of a German story by Christoph von Schmid. THE EASTER FIRES OF FREDERICKSBURG, adapted from various sources and from 'Pancakes and Painted Eggs' by Jean Chapman, © 1981, published by Hodder and Stoughton.

Page 68: FORTY HOURS, FORTY DAYS, FORTY YEARS, based on 'The Sunday Sermons of the Great Fathers' compiled by Rev. M. F. Toal.

Pages 69-71: THE SELFISH GIANT, adapted and abridged from 'The Selfish Giant' in a book of stories by Oscar Wilde, published in 1888.

Pages 74-76: THE EASTER TREE, an original story © Mala Powers.

Pages 77-79: EASTER SYMBOLS, an original collection © Mala Powers, includes THE LAMB, a poem by William Blake and FLOWERS, a stanza from 'Easter Time', a poem by Laura E. Richards.

Pages 80-81: WHEN THE ROOT CHILDREN WAKE UP, translated and adapted from a story by Helen Dean Fish in a picture book by Sibylle V. Olfers, American edition published by J. P. Lippincott Co.

Page 83: THE FEAST OF EOSTRE, adapted from a story by Martha Knapp in 'Highlights for Children', © 1974; used with permission of the publisher.

Pages 84-85: A LESSON OF FAITH, adapted from a story by Margaret Gatty in 'The Easter Book of Legends and Stories', (ed) Hazeltine and Smith, copyright 1947 Lothrop, Lee and Shepard; used with permission.

Pages 87-90: HOLY WEEK, based on the Gospels of Matthew, Mark, Luke and John, includes DEAR DONKEY, an original poem by Mala Powers, and THE ROBIN AND THE THORNS, an Irish legend.

Page 91: EASTER IS, selected stanzas from 'Easter Is', a poem by Mrs. Paul E. King in the Easter issue of Ideal Magazine, Vol, 39, No. 2 © 1982; used with permission.

Pages 92-93: THE MAID OF EMMAUS, adapted from a story by Agnes Sligh Turnbull in 'The Easter Book of Legends and Stories', (ed) Hazeltine and Smith, copyright 1947 Lothrop, Lee and Shepard; used with permission.

Page 94: THE DAYS AFTER EASTER and THE GREAT EASTER EGG DILEMMA OF 1877!, adapted from 'Children's Story' by Mala Powers, © 1979.

Page 95: THE WELCOME, adapted from 'A Slavonic Easter Legend', an English translation, in Cresset Magazine; used with permission of the publishers, Camphill Publications Inc.

Page 97: ASCENSIONTIDE, based on The Acts of the Apostles and the Gospel of Matthew, includes a stanza from 'The Sacred Songs of Novalis', translated from the German.

Page 98: AQUA AND HER SISTERS, adapted from 'Aqua — the Raindrop' by Richard H. Lewis; used with the permission of the author.

Page 100: THE LIGHT OF THE SUN, a translation of a poem by Rudolf Steiner in 'The Keys of the Kingdom', published by Rudolf Steiner Press.

Page 101: THE EARLIEST CHRISTIAN CHURCH, based on The Acts of the Apostles Chapters 1 and 2.

Page 110: THE MIRACLE OF MONTE SANT' ANGELO, based on 'The Golden Legend' by Jacopus de Voragine, a 13th century Italian scholar.

Page 111: THE CROWD WITHIN, the first stanza by an anonymous author, the second stanza an original work © Mala Powers.

Pages 112-113: ST. GEORGE AND THE DRAGON, based on English, French and Russian legends. AS THE DRAGON IS SLAIN, based on 'The Golden Legend' by Jacopus de Voragine, a 13th century Italian scholar.

Page 114: ANGELS! ANGELS! EVERYWHERE; the Christian nomenclature of the Spiritual Hierarchies is attributed to Dionysius the Areopagite, a disciple of the Apostle Paul.

Page 115: LUCIFER'S JEWEL AND THE HOLY GRAIL, based on Celtic and French legends.

Pages 116-117: LEGENDS OF THE HOLY GRAIL and THE QUEST FOR THE HOLY GRAIL, © Mala Powers, original stories based on 'Idylls of the King' by Alfred, Lord Tennyson and 'Le Morte Darthur' by Thomas Malory.

Pages 118-119: ALL HALLOWS' TIDE, © Mala Powers, based on Celtic customs. THE LAND OF MEMORY, an adaptation based on 'The Blue Bird' by Maurice Maeterlinck.

All selections within FOLLOW THE YEAR not credited or acknowledged by author, publisher or origin are original works and copyrighted herein by Mala Powers.

All possible care and effort have been taken to make full and proper acknowledgements for use of every selection under copyright. Errors which have accidentally occurred, or sources not properly or duly acknowledged, will be corrected in future printing, provided proper notice is sent to the publisher.

Suggested Reading for Christian Holidays

A CELEBRATION OF CHRISTMAS, (ed) Gillian Cooke, Queen Anne Press, 1980

CHRISTMAS IN RITUAL AND TRADITION, CHRISTIAN AND PAGAN, Clement A. Miles, T. F. Unwin, 1912

CHRISTMAS STORIES ROUND THE WORLD, (ed) Lois E. Johnson, Frederick Warne and Co., 1970

FOLLOW THE STAR, Mala Powers, Hodder and Stoughton, 1981

THE STORY OF THE OTHER WISE MAN, Henry Van Dyke, Harper & Row, 1983

WHY THE CHIMES RANG AND OTHER STORIES, Raymond Macdonald Alden, Collins, 1948

EASTER, Cass R. Sandak, Franklin Watts, 1980

PANCAKES AND PAINTED EGGS, Jean Chapman, Hodder and Stoughton Australia, 1981

THE LIGHT BEYOND THE FOREST, (Arthurian Legends), Rosemary Sutcliff, The Bodley Head, 1979

ANGELS: GOD'S SECRET AGENTS, Billy Graham, Hodder and Stoughton, 1977

BRITISH FOLKLORE, Mark Alexander, Weidenfeld and Nicholson Ltd, 1982

CATHERINE MARSHALL'S STORY BIBLE, Hodder and Stoughton, 1982

FESTIVALS, FAMILY AND FOOD, Diana Carey and Judy Large, Hawthorne Press, 1983

HERE'S THE YEAR, Peter Watkins and Erica Hughes, Julia MacRae Books, 1981